WE CALLED OURSELVES ROCKETBOATMEN:

The Untold Stories of the
Top-Secret LCS(S) Rocket Boat Missions of World War II
at Sicily, Normandy (Omaha and Utah Beaches), and Southern France

The events, people, and places herein are depicted to the best recollection of the author, who assumes complete and sole responsibility for the accuracy of this narrative.

We Called Ourselves Rocketboatmen

The Untold Stories of the Top-Secret LCS(S) Rocket Boat Missions of World War II at Sicily, Normandy (Omaha and Utah Beaches), and Southern France

Copyright © 2018 by William Howard Palmer Jr.

Library of Congress Control Number: 2021903384
ISBN-13:   Paperback: 978-1-64749-373-8
             ePub: 978-1-64749-374-5

Printed in the United States of America

GoToPublish LLC
1-888-337-1724
www.gotopublish.com
info@gotopublish.com

WE CALLED OURSELVES ROCKETBOATMEN:

The Untold Stories of the
Top-Secret LCS(S) Rocket Boat Missions of World War II
at Sicily, Normandy (Omaha and Utah Beaches), and Southern France

Ensign Albert M. Low

"My crew and I feared we'd die; yet such premonitions were seldom vented,
and we didn't let fear interfere with duty."

Ensign Albert M. Low, Southern France

Commendation, Utah Beach, 6 objectives destroyed
Silver Star, Southern France, Blue Beach
Purple Heart, Southern France, Blue Beach

DEDICATION AND ACKNOWLEDGMENT

This book is dedicated to the brave men who manned the newly Top Secret LCS(S) "Rocket Boat" Missions in the European Theatre of World War Two at the Invasions of Sicily, July 1943; Invasion of Normandy, June 6, 1944 (Omaha and Utah Beaches); and Invasion of Southern France, August 1944. In all cases they preceded the first waves of soldiers with rocket bombardment and machine gun support from the small 36' LCS(S)—(Landing Craft Support, Small).

The two unique elements of their untold story is that they were (1) the first offensive boats to attack the beaches at close range less than 300 yards from the beach one half hour before the first wave of soldiers in LCVPs landed, and (2) they were the first small boats of any navy in the world to deliver rockets at a land based enemy. Their heroic stories have never been formally told.

May the full story of their bravery and heroism now come to light to be documented and never forgotten. May we pass it on to Naval History, to our children, grandchildren and posterity.

I thank all of you who contributed to this compilation.

Special thanks goes to the Ensign Albert M. Low family: Albert, Pete, and Patricia for the contribution of their father's highly documented heroic stories. His Rocket Boat missions into Utah and Southern France beaches provided a powerful backdrop to several chapters of this book.

CONTENTS

INTRODUCTION

William H. Palmer

As previously stated, the Top Secret Rocket Boat Missions have never been formally told. Even in 1994, at the heralded 50 Year Anniversary of D-Day, the *Chicago Tribune,* which summarized the navies' first steps of the Invasion below omits any involvement of the LCS(S) Rocket Boats leading role.

Chicago Tribune June 6th 1994—Notice L/R: Landing Craft; Attack Transport, LSTs, LCTs, LCIs, LCVPs right to the beach but no mention of the LCS(S) Rocket Boat leading the LCVPs with Rocket Bombardment and Gunnery:

Staging area for Allied attack transports
Transports reached the unloading area at 2:30 a.m. June 6. From here, landing craft made their 11-mile trip shoreward to assigned departure lines. There they circled and waited for H-Hour.

Transport unloading area: About 20 miles across

Allied sea lanes: Convoy routes for Allied task forces.

Dixie line: Forward line of unloading area, 11 miles offshore.

NORMANDY

Landing craft
Smaller Coast Guard LCVPs from assault transports carried 30-32 troops each and brought the first waves of troops ashore. Larger LCIs followed, each carrying 200 assault troops. LSTs carrying 300 men and 60 vehicles and LCTs that carried 55 men and 11 vehicles were among the 1,426 landing and beaching craft.

Barrage balloons: Protected vessels from low-flying German aircraft.

German defenses: Beach obstacles, mines, tank traps, machine guns and artillery.

LSTs   LCTs   LCIs   LCVPs

Landing craft departure lines: 2-4,000 yards offshore

Beaches: About 300 yards wide.

Nor is there any mention of the Rock Boat Mission at 6:00 a.m. in the time summary of early June 6. This time chronology should include 6:00 a.m. – LCS(S) Rocket Boats approach Omaha and Utah Beaches with rocket barrages to prep beaches for LCVP troop landings.

5:30 a.m.: German coastal gun batteries begin sporadic firing, unaware of the magnitude of the invasion.

5:50 a.m.: Allied naval bombardment begins, detonating large German minefields and destroying many German beach defenses and inland targets. Heavy and medium fighter bombers also attack targets.

6:30 a.m.: Landing on Omaha and Utah beaches (U.S. forces).
7:25 a.m.: Landing on Gold and Sword beaches (British forces).

However, the LCS(S) Rocket Boat Missions had not totally been omitted from history—Just after D-Day in August of 1944, National Geographic featured an article on the "Landing Craft for the Invasion," in which every type of small boat was listed with their functions. Briefly on page 5 it mentions LCS(S) Rocket Boats and their role during the invasion on the greatest day of World War Two. It states, "LCS(S)s are small support boats firing rockets and machine guns."

The National Geographic Magazine

However, the picture from page 6 shows what might be seen looking back toward the troop carrier LCVPs as they lead with Rockets and Machine Gunnery.

This picture is so close up you don't get the full perspective of the perils and duties of the LCS(S) Rocket Boat Missions.

U. S. Coast Guard, Official

This Is What the Enemy Sees When the First Wave Hits the Beach

From the bow of an LCS(S) (Landing Craft, Support, Small), the combat photographer looks back at assault boats, or LCVPs, speeding shoreward, loaded with troops. Accompanied by shelling, strafing, and bombing with live ammunition, these maneuvers on the eastern United States coast simulate invasion. In battle, the men crouch down behind the armored visor and fire rockets from the covered projector at right. Cruisers in the distance cover the landing with shellfire.

Finally, the picture on page ten, even though distant, portrays the true nature of the LCS(S) Rocket Boats Mission having preceded the first wave, fired their Rockets onto the beach at Eniwetok (Asiatic Theatre), and then heading back, leaving smoke screens and greeting the first wave of soldiers in LCVPs on the way back.

I have concluded there are several reasons for the omission of the LCS(S) Rocket Boat Program and their role from history. The first reason is that concentration on the LCS(S) Rocket Boat program lasted only about 30 months before it was replaced with more advanced effective technology. There were only 150 of the type 1; LCS(S) Rocket Boats with rocket racks parallel to the deck (ex. Page 3 and only 408 type 2; LCS(S) Rocket Boats with rocket rackets set back in a well on a 40 degree angle to avoid misfires into the bow of the boat (ex. Page 9). This was a total of 558 LCS(S) Rocket Boats ever manufactured. (See Admiral Kings small boat totals below.) It was a short lived program with a few number of boats manufactured and deployed.

The second reason for the omission from history is that the Rocket Boats all being deployed from different transports, having completed their missions, all went back to their separate transports, and the original Officers of these Rocket Boats and crews never united again after the War, as all other major crews of Transports and LSTs, Destroyers and Carriers do. They had no common boat to unite around, thus no annual get together; no capability of easily finding each other, as there is today via the Internet.

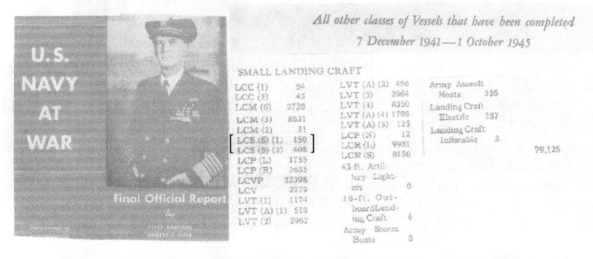

My original investigation of my father, Ensign William H. Palmer's D-Day Mission started in reverse. I contacted two annual reunion members of a larger ship, LST 285, who my father was with in 1945 on his Pacific cleanup of the Japanese Islands, Frank Shea; Radio Man and Ken Izzo; plankholders of LST285.

LST285 in 1945 at end of Pacific Tour

Ken Izzo; Yeoman, William Palmer Jr., Frank Shea; Radioman
Two Members of LST285's Crew

Communications with Frank Shea and Ken Izzo led me to the conclusion that my father was not on LST285 on D-Day. This led me to further review of his exact orders and the contact of his coxswain of his small British Wooden Sea Plane Tender on D-Day; Mario Preato, who said, "I took Officer Palmer into with 300 ^{feet} of Utah Beach and he swam in with whatever messages he had to deliver," and his new assigned operation for D-Day no longer Rocket Boats. This Operation, Task Force K, had never been formally told either and research and contact with living members of the 48 men assigned to Task Force K; Dispatch Boats of Force "O" who relayed all major communications to the beachheads during 21 days of Radio Blackout. Their story was courageous, and in 2005 I completed the Book *48 Brave Men*.

"48 Brave Men"
Dispatch Boats of Force "O"
front cover

Ensign William H. Palmer

"48 Brave Men"
back cover

Having completed this book about my father, Ensign William H. Palmer, "48 Brave Men" with Charles S. Reder as Commanding Officer of Task Force K, I then decided to try to research the Operation he was originally trained for: D-Day; the LCS(S) Rocket Boat Program.

I started with Lt. Commander Charles S. Reder who had participated a year earlier in the Rocket Boat missions at the Invasion of Sicily. He provided his diary from Sicily and an original Rocket Boat Invasion Map of Sicily. This was to be his only Rocket boat mission being transferred to Task Force K (mentioned above in *48 Brave Men* synopsis). He led me to his buddy Ensign Roscoe C. DuMond who also went into Sicily with his rocket Boat and finally Southern France. Roscoe provided his diary from Sicily and an original Rocket Boat Deployment Map of Southern France.

Next, to my surprise, many of the Omaha and Utah Beach participants were still alive. Ensigns Edwin Lemkin, Nick Zuras and Herman Vorel from Omaha Beach were my first contacts. Then Lemuel C. Laney who went into Utah Beach across from <u>Stoke Holmes, Yogi Berra's Officer and to my surprise, Yogi Berra himself, who played a major Rocket Boat role at Utah Beach as a gunner on D-Day June 6th, 1944 and Southern France August 15th, 1944</u>. Ensign Albert M. Low perhaps leading the most aggressive of the Rocket Boat Crews whose summaries at Utah Beach and Southern France were inimitable. This compelled me to bestow on them the name "The Quintessential Rocket Boat Crew" because of their valor in taking out so many enemy fortifications at Utah Beach and Southern France while under enemy fire; three members of the crew having sustained machine gun wounds and recipients of Purple Hearts.

When all my research was was completed, I was fortunate to have the support of my favorite New York Yankee of all time; Yogi Berra.

"Nobody knew about rocket boats. We were a secret mission as part of the invasion. We moved quick, shot rockets 300 yards from the shore, and didn't have time to be scared. It was some experience and Bill Palmer captures what we experienced." – Yogi Berra

Additional Media on 1st Mission D-Day "Rocket Boats"
Radio Interview with Derik Glen of WVLT 92.1 on USS New Jersey April 20, 2013

Pictured L/R - Jasck Willard, Marketing Director: USS N.J. - Rocket Boat Officer, Ensign Nick Zuras of Omaha Beach - Author: William H. Palmer "Rockerboatmen" - Phillip Rowan, Executive Director: USS N.J.

NBC "Rocket Boat" Interview June 4th 2012

NBC Anchor, Chuck Scarborough - Rocket Boat Officer; Enisgn Nick Zuras (95), Omaha Beach - Author, William H. Palmer; "We Called Ourselves Rocketboatmen" - you can view this NBC interview and live Rocketboat film footage on my Youtube channel: "We Called Ourselves Rocektboatmen".

01718

8 1437

ELEVENTH AMPHIBIOUS FORCE

11thPhib/A16-3
Serial: 00950

17 AUG 1944

FIRST ENDORSEMENT to:
ComPhibsUKAY Secret
ltr. A16-3/(05/Hr)
Serial: 001748 of
5 August 1944.

From: Commander Assault Force "O".
To : Commander-in-Chief, United States Fleet.

Subject: Action Report of 4 LCS(S) carried by LST 374 in Assault on COLLEVILLE-VIERVILLE Sector, Coast of NORMANDY.

1. Forwarded.

2. The 48 rockets which can be fired in two loadings of the projectors aboard the LCS(S) constitutes a weapon of considerable power. Because of its armament and its ability to close the beach it is considered to be capable of furnishing valuable close support. No other type of small craft requires more intensive training of personnel, however. Whenever a number of LSC(S)'s are to be used together in an operation, their training should be joint and should cover a considerable period of time. They should be manned by personnel who are aggressive, resourceful, imaginative and daring. Well handled, LCS(S)'s can upon occasion be very effective. Indifferently handled, they are not worth the davit space they take away from LCVPs.

J. L. Hall Jr

J. L. HALL, Jr.

Copy to:
ComPhibsUKAY
LST 374

COMMANDER-IN-CHIEF
FLAG OFFICE
RECEIVED
1944 AUG 25 10 33

CHAPTER 1

Introduced to the Top Secret Nature
of our LCS(S) Rocket
Boat Program

Ltjg. Charles S. Reder, Ensigns Albert M. Low & Harry W. Tennant

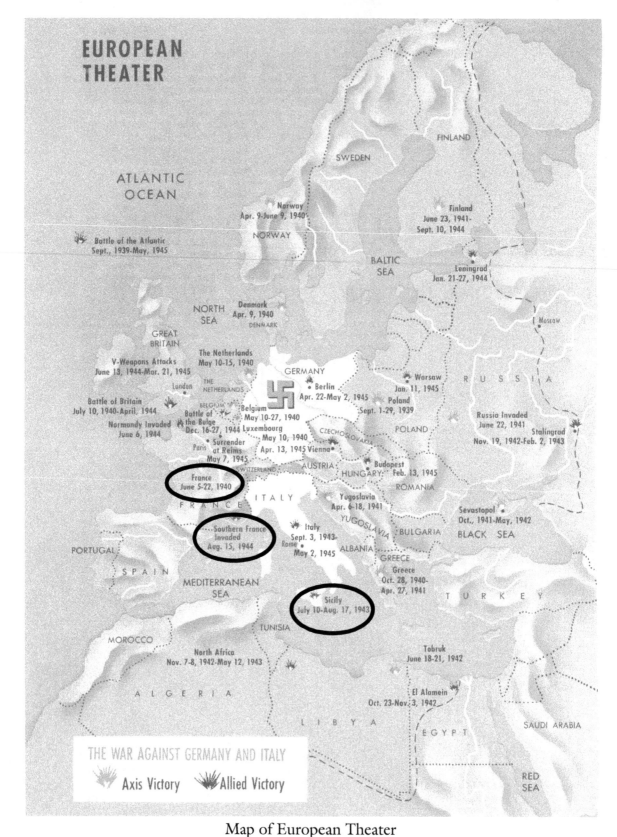

Map of European Theater
LCS(S) Rocket Boat Missions at Sicily, 1943, Normandy; Northern France, June 6, 1944, Southern France, August 1944

Introduced to the Top Secret Nature of our LCS(S) Rocket Boat Program
by Ltjg. Charles S. Reder

Ltjg. Charles Simons Reder

Entered the USN in 1942 in Pittsfield, MA. Signed up for flight training, but was turned down because he was color blind. Was placed in the newly top secret LCS(S) Rocket Boat Program. Participated in one of the first of the Rocket Boat missions in Gela, Sicily, July 1943.

How I was introduced to the Highly Secret Rocket Boat Program
Diary of Ltjg. Charles Simons Reder; April 1–2, 1943;

I have been placed in charge of five other officers and 30 men and we are going to Solomons, MD, near Washington, D.C., to train in special type boats. This base is fine—only 60 miles from Washington. I'm enthused about our new boats. They are called "Support Boats"; like a PT boat, but shoot 30 lb. rockets. Purpose is to go in before landing craft to 150 yards off shore and wipe out machine gun nests, etc. The officer in charge of the boat has a five man crew.

LCS(S) Rocket Boat Training (Chesapeake Bay, Norfolk, VA, and Solomons, MD, April 1943) Notice the rocket racks on both sides and 12 smoke pots at the stern.
Picture taken while on maneuvers at Solomons, MD, 1943, by Ltjg. Charles S. Reder Identified: Ltjg Richard F. O'Meara standing center of ship of a Type 1 Rocket Boat (rocket racks parallel to deck).

Introduced to the Top Secret Nature of Our LCS(S) Rocket Boat Program
Ensign Albert M. Low

The War Room

Ensign Albert M. Low

Shortly after training at Little Creek, six of us ensigns were marched into a war room, cautioned that what we'd be seeing was top secret, and that violation of this trust could extend to a General Courts Martial. We were then introduced to invasion procedures by way of an artist's rendering of ships and small boats assembled on an 8 x 24 foot piece of canvas-covered plywood.

Our group of officers gathered around as the instructor ran the planned invasion procedure. Small, heavily armed boats would fire onto the beaches to clear them. The beaches would be stormed by troops brought by mini boats, both having earlier arrived on transports convoyed to within ten miles of the hostile territory at Normandy Beach.

**base model LCS(S)
Rocket Boat**
Time Magazine Dec, 1943

Step by step the invasion procedures were explained and demonstrated. The attack was run a second time. Still we were not told what our duty would be. After reviewing yet again what we had seen, the instructor asked us which boats would most likely be ravished by enemy firepower. All agreed that the boats that led the first wave, supporting the invading soldiers with machine gun fire and rockets, would be the ones to catch hell!

"That's correct, gentleman. You will be commanding these things." He picked a model off the board and held it high, saying "The proper name is LCS(S) or Landing Craft Support, Small. If you think you can't stand up to it, say so now!"

Apparently nobody wanted out.

He continued, "The cockpit is armor plated. The boat carries twin fifty-caliber machine guns, two thirty-caliber machine guns, twelve smoke pots, and two rocket racks, each capable of holding twenty-four rockets." He paused. "That's right, gentleman, they fire rockets. As far as we know, these will be the only boats in the navies of the world throwing rockets at a land-based enemy. At present, the plan is for twenty-four boats with a like number of crew and officers. Gentlemen, I promise, you will see duty under fire!"

(continued on Page 8)

Front view of Rocket Boat Bridge Showing twin 50 Calibers
Rear View of Rocket Boat Bridge showing 2 – 30 Calibers

Ensign Cranwell's Rocket Boat Crew, L/R: Ensign Albert B. Cranwell; w/binoculars, George Hartley; gunner, Rt—Robert Holley; motormac, Malvin Schoenfeld; Joseph Johnson; Theophile Pidgeon. Pictures submitted by daughter Elizabeth Cranwell

Introduced to the Top Secret Nature of our LCS(S) Rocket Boat Program
by Ensign Harry W. Tennant

Ensign Harry W. Tennant

While in training in Rocketry at Solomons MD, Reder's group (all of us—24 officers and 144 enlisted men) mustered beside a railroad car, and heard for the first time why we were there. A naval officer stood in the doorway of the rail car with a rocket in hand, our first knowledge and use of this secret weapon. The officer had the full attention of us all, so he described the rocket weapon, its handling and safety characteristics and that it was to be fired from Rocket Boats LCS(S)s at close range on German enemy defending the French beaches. The LCS(S) boats were to be the first wave, ahead of landing personnel, and we were to damage the enemy beach fortifications and enable our U.S. forces to land and capture beachheads. Each LCS(S) would have 48 rockets, each rocket equivalent to a Destroyer 6" shell, plus machine guns. The LCS(S) would have heavy side armor and a heavy cone to protect its crew. We were then issued the rockets and loaded—armed training LCS(S) boats and scheduled an exercise to approach and fire our rockets on Solomons Island. We were all attentive and followed training exactly. The exercise went well and we were permitted to go ashore to see the damages and results of our Rocket barrages. While on shore to view the rocket damage, two enlisted men found an unexploded rocket and started back to the beach water edge where our LCS(S) boats were sitting. Fortunately, one of our officers recognized the danger of handling this unexploded rocket and very carefully brought them to a LCVP craft that was on hand. The rocket was carried very carefully on board, holding in same position on their shoulders, while the boat went out to deep water, and the unexploded rocket was dropped overboard. It sank to the bottom and exploded, rupturing the LCVP bottom. Following this event, everyone was most attentive to safety.

Ensign Herman Vorel's LCS(S) Rocket Boat Crew on bridge of Rocket Boat
Displaying, Left, Barrage Rocket
Right, Smoke Rocket

From Solomons, MD, we were put on a train in locked passenger cars under heavy secrecy arrangements to travel to Navy Base Long Island to await orders to England. No photographers, newsman were allowed to photograph nor witness our highly secret LCS(S) Program while training in the states. Next we convoyed to Plymouth, England Naval Base. In Plymouth waters we trained for D-Day aboard the Rocket Boats.

CHAPTER 2

Rocket Boats vs PT Boats

Ensigns Albert M. Low & Harry W. Tennant

Rocket Boats vs PT Boats
Ensign Albert M. Low

The War Room, continued from Page 4:

All eyes fixed on the model. Neptune might have sculpted such a toy to give Triton, his son. From that time on, we called our boats "Rocket boats," and ourselves "Rocket boat officers."

Anticipation energized my body as I gazed at the model. Her lines were like a PTs, but more compact and infinitely more warlike. The differences were abundantly clear: we were to carry rockets rather than torpedoes, and we were to stand and fight. Compared to the PT with its superior speed, built for hit and run, our speed amounted to standing still.

LCS(S) Rocket Boat 36' base model; Time Magazine August 1944

LCS(S) Rocket Boats 36' vs PT Boat 80'
Max Speed: Rocket Boats, 12 mph/PT boats, 30 mph

We watched, paying silent, awed attention as the commanding officer detailed our boat's design and its crew's duties.

Features of the rocket boat:
1. Armor plated cockpit
2. Smoke pot racks (12)
3. Center ship's twin 50-caliber machine guns
4. 30-caliber machine guns (2)
5. Rocket racks (2), each with 24 rocket capacity

Crewmen and duties:
6. Boatswain's mate (BM2c)—functioned as helmsman (coxswain, cox); subject to his officer's authority, he ran the boat
7. Gunners mate (GM2c, fireman)—maintained the machine guns, smoke pots, ammunition; his battle station was in the twin fifty machine gun assembly cradle, located mid-ship.
8. Signalman (SM)—in charge of all communication; used hand signal, and flags during the day, lanterns at night, when there was one, also tended the radio
9. Motor machinist (MoMM2c)—took care of diesel engines and mechanical systems.
10. Two Seaman (S2c), loaded rockets and manned the 30-caliber machine guns, stood lookout, handled lines, kept the boat shipshape

Rocket Boat Crew of Ensign Roscoe C. DuMond

Stealth—Rocket Boats ran too shallow to be torpedoed, were too small to be hit by German artillery; 88 mm; had too much machine gunnery to be matched from 300–500 yards away. Ensign Harry W. Tennant

CHAPTER 3

1943, First Successful LCS(S) Rocket Boat Deployments at
Invasions of Sicily, Italy July 10, 1943 and Salerno
September 3, 1943

Ltjg. Charles S. Reder, Ensigns Roscoe C. DuMond & Robert H. Goldsmith

Ens. Robert H. Goldsmith   *Ltjg. Charles Simons Reder*   *Ens. Roscoe C. DuMond*

Invasion of Sicily

Allied Invasion of Sicily
The Allied invasion of Sicily began on the night of July 9–10, 1943 and ended August 17 in an Allied victory. The invasion of the island was codenamed "Operation Husky" and it launched the Italian Campaign. Husky was the largest amphibious operation of World War II up to that time, in terms of men landed on the beaches and of frontage.

Planning
In the early part of 1943, following the conclusion that, the Invasion of France would be impossible that year; it was decided to use troops from the recently won North African Campaign to invade the Island of Sicily. The strategic goals were to remove the island as a base for Axis shipping and aircraft, allowing free passage to Allied ships in the Mediterranean Sea, and put pressure on the regime of Benito Mussolini in the hope of eventually having Italy struck from the war. The attempt to knock Italy out of the war failed, as popular anti-German sentiment boiled over and overthrew Mussolini and joined the war on the side of the Western Allies. However, it could also act as a precursor to the Invasion of Italy, although this was not agreed by the Allies at the time of the Invasion, the Americans in particular resisting commitment to any operation that might conceivably delay the Invasion of France.

Four airborne operations were carried out, landing during the night of July 9–10, as part of the invasion; two were British and two American. The American troops were from the 82nd Airborne Division, making their first combat parachute jump. The strong winds blew the dropping aircraft off course and scattered them widely; the result was that around half the U.S. paratroopers failed to make it to their rallying points. British glider-land troops fared little better; only 12 out of 144 gliders landing on target, many in the sea. Nevertheless, the scattered airborne troops maximized their opportunities, attacking patrols and creating confusion wherever possible.

The sea landings, despite the weather, were carried out against little opposition, the Italian units stationed on the shoreline lacking equipment and transport. The British walked into the port of Syracuse virtually unopposed. Only in the American Centre at Gela was a substantial counter-attack made, at exactly the point where the U.S. Airborne were supposed to have been. On July 11, Patton ordered his reserve parachute regiments to drop and reinforce the centre. Unfortunately, not every unit had been informed of the drop, and the transports, which arrived shortly after an Axis air raid, were fired on by the Royal Navy, losing 37 out of 144 planes to friendly fire.

Consequences and Aftermath
The casualties on the Axis side totaled 29,000, with 144,000 captured. The U.S. losses were 2,237 killed and 6,544 wounded and captured; the British suffered 2,721 dead and 10,122 wounded and captured; the Canadians suffered 2,320 casualties, including 562 killed in action. For many of the American forces, this was their first time in combat. However, the Axis successfully evacuated 100,000 men and 10,000 vehicles from Sicily, which the Allies were unable to prevent rescuing such a large number of troops from the threat of capture, representing a major success for the Axis.

Strategically, the Sicilian Operation achieved the goals set out by Allied Planners. Axis air and naval forces were driven from the Island, the Mediterranean Sea lanes were opened, and Mussolini had been toppled from power. It opened the way for the Allied Invasion of Italy.

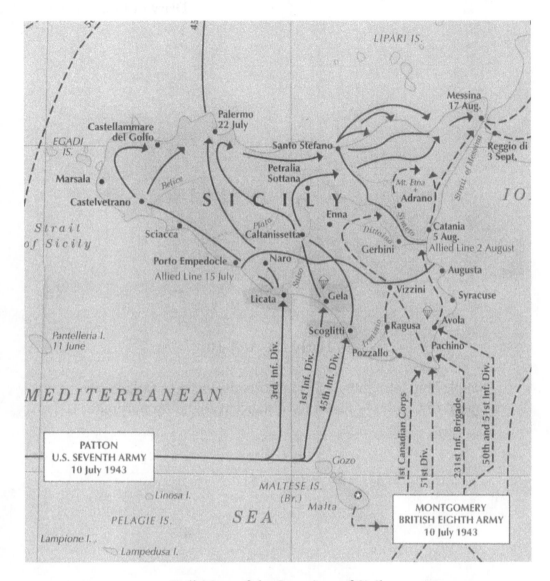

Full Map of the Invasion of Sicily

American landings were from the southern side of the Island at Licata, Gela, Scoglitti. British Landings were from the West side as documented above. The Axis main counter attack was at Gela. Both Ltjg. Charles Simons Reder and Ensign Roscoe DuMond debarking from the USS Harry Lee and 4 other Ensigns from the USS Leonard Wood convened with their Rocket Boats at a center point of debarkation and led (preceded) the first wave of infantry with the offensive strikes of their LCS(S) Rocket Boats assuring (softening the beach head with their 48 rockets).

The following pages are the collection of original LCS(S) Rocket Boat Plan and Map and diaries of Ltjg. Charles S. Reder, Roscoe DuMond, and Robert Goldsmith, pertaining to this first Rocket Boat Mission at Gela Sicily.

May 11, 1943

The big day. DuMond and I have been ordered to report to the USS Harry Lee with our crews. Poole, McMahon to the USS Andromeda, Selig and Hoffman to the USS Ohara.

Diary of Ltjg. Charles S. Reder

USS Harry Lee APA-10

Simple Ship Sketchings of Transports deployed to Gela, Sicily given to Charles S. Reder for distance recognition purposes

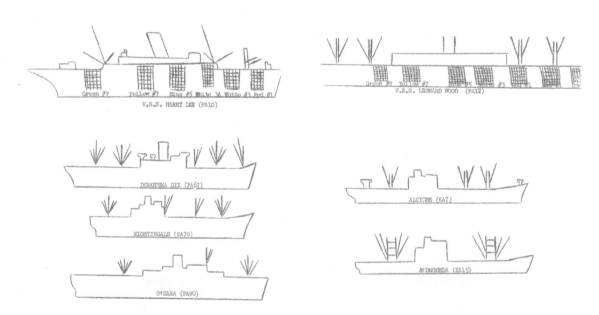

Headed for Sicily, Thursday July 2, 1943

Had a meeting the morning in which we saw pictures, maps of the beach and very close detailed photographs showing pillboxes etc. On the afternoon our Support Boat Division had

a meeting over at MEK on the Calvert. We trained our actual boat employment and everything looks swell. Met with boat crew and got everything squared away.
Diary of Ensign Robert H. Goldsmith

Actual copy of Ensign Robert H. Goldsmith's Diary July 1–2, 1943

Ensign Robert H. Goldsmith

Born: August 15, 1920 in Binghamton, NY
Graduated: Northwestern and Wharton Business Schools,
Harvard Business School
Occupation: Executive with Cole National Corp.
Spouse: Francine Bailys, May 2, 1950, had two sons
Passed away: November 14, 1995

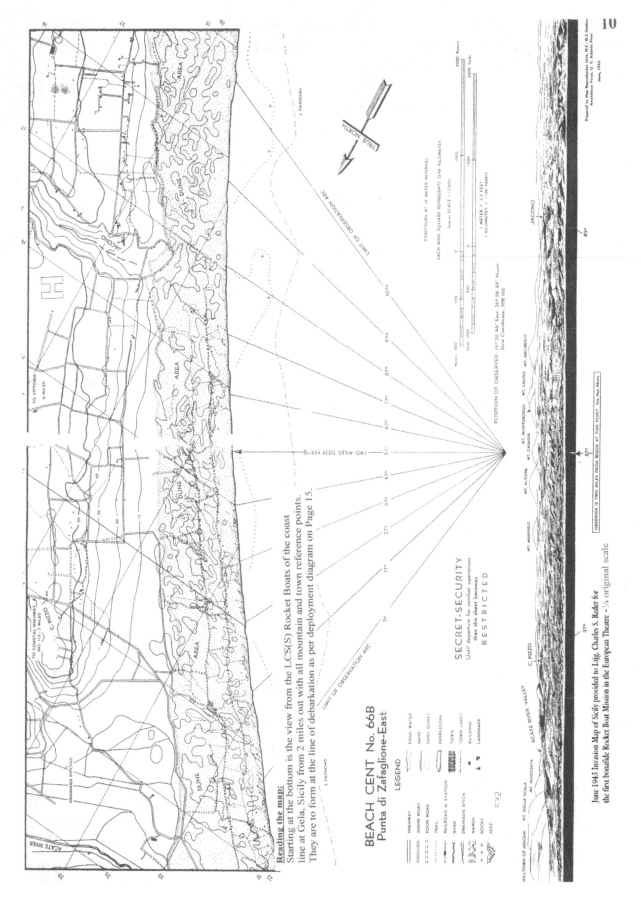

Reading the map:

Starting at the bottom is the view from the LCS(S) Rocket Boats of the coast line at Gela, Sicily from 2 miles out with all mountain and town reference points. They are to form at the line of debarkation as per deployment diagram on Page 15.

BEACH CENT No. 66B
Punta di Zafaglione–East

LEGEND

HIGHWAY		FOUL WATER	
GOOD ROAD		SAND	
POOR ROAD		SAND DUNES	
TRAIL		DEPRESSION	
RAILROAD & STATION		TOWN	
RIVER		TOWN LIMITS	
DRAINAGE DITCH		BUILDING	
MARSH		LANDMARK	
ROCKS			
REEF	6·22		

SECRET–SECURITY
Until departure for combat operations
then this sheet becomes
RESTRICTED

CONTOURS AT ·10 METER INTERVAL.

EACH GRID SQUARE REPRESENTS ONE KILOMETER.

Approx. SCALE 1:17,000

1 METER = 3.3 FEET
1 KILOMETER = 1100 YARDS

POSITION OF OBSERVER - 14° 20′ 45″ East, 36° 56′ 45″ North
Grid Coordinate: 308 168.

TRUE NORTH

June 1943 Invasion Map of Sicily provided to Ltjg. Charles S. Reder for
the first bonafide Rocket Boat Mission in the European Theatre – ¼ original scale

LCS(S) Rocket Boat Plan at Sicily, July 1943

The following 6 pages are the actual Rocket Boat orders and strategy and diagrams to be deployed by Ltjg. Charles S. Reder and Ensign Roscoe C. DuMond at Gela, Sicily.

Sub-Order of Operation Order 4–43
Support Boat Employment Plan

Ltjg. Charles S. Reder

Ensign Roscoe C. DuMond and LCS(S) Crew

ANNEX LOVE TO COMMANDER TASK UNIT EIGHT FIVE POINT ONE POINT TWO

OPERATION ORDER 4 - 43

SUPPORT BOAT EMPLOYMENT PLAN

Reference: Chapter 15, Annex SUGAR, Force General Order No. 1.

1.   LCS(S) will be employed in accordance with the doctrine laid down in the reference, with the exceptions listed below. The paragraphs given refer to corresponding paragraphs in the reference.

1. LCS(S) will carry 42 barrage rockets, 6 smoke rockets, 8 smoke pots H.C. Mark III, 5 smoke floats Mark IV, 2 velocity power cable cutters.

2(a) There will be no rocket firing in the Transport or Rendezvous Area. Such firing would endanger own Fire Support Destroyers.

2(c) There will be no machine gun or rocket firing on the beach by LCS(S) after the troops have landed.

2(g) Not employed during this landing.

5(a) Each Support Boat load rockets as follows: in the starboard projector, 12 barrage rockets; in the port projector, 9 rockets in the top three rails and 3 smoke rockets in the bottom rail.

5(d) Modify as follows: Support Boats will commence ranging salvos about 1200 yards from the beach. The Beach Marking Boat should be stationed at this point. Support Boat Division Commanders only, will fire ranging salvos of 3 rockets each. Each LCS(S) observe closely the fall of shot. When it appears that the Support Boat Division Commanders have the range to the beach, (i.e. that rockets are falling on the beach and not in the water) all LCS(S) commence firing of salvos of 3 rockets per LCS(S) according to the schedule shown below:

TIME SCHEDULE	ROUNDS FIRED
H minus 5	3
(5 minutes after leaving Line of Departure)	
H minus 4 1/2	6
H minus 4	9
H minus 3 1/2	12
H minus 3	15
H minus 2 1/2	18
H minus 2	21
H minus 1 1/2	3 smoke

L-1

Monday July 5, 1943

All day we watched the ships pull into the harbor. The skipper announced that this is D-Day −5 and that 500,000 troops and 2,500 vessels are taking part as well as 5,000 planes.

Diary of Ensign Robert H. Goldsmith

Sicily, July 9, 1943

Spent the morning assembling the Rockets. There is rough weather and 45-mile-per-hour wind. It's now 2100 and won't be long before the big show begins.

Diary of Ensign Robert H. Goldsmith

LANDING OPERATION ORDERS

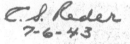

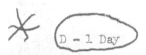

D - 1 Day

1900   Swing out the following boats and lash securely at the rail: LCVP's 1, 2, 3, 4, 12. LCP(R)'s 6, 7, 8, 9, 10, 11. LCS(S)14.

2000   Stream paravanes.

2200   Midnight lunch only for crews of the following boats: 1, 2, 3, 4, 9, 11, 12, [13, 14,] 15 and T.L. #2. Third Division provide reliefs at gun and lookout stations for members of those crews prior to this time. Coxswain of each of these boats draw sandwiches and coffee for his crew at this time. (51 men and 2 officers total)

2245   Set Condition 4.

2300 (about) Lower boats 1, 2, 3, 4, 9, 11, 12, [13, 14,] 15 and T.L. #2. (2nd Division lower Support Boats first)
LCVP's 1, 2, 3, 4, 12, 15 report to the USS LEONARD WOOD (PA12), join assembly circle on her starboard quarter. Each boat leaves the ship as soon as it is lowered and proceeds independently. Do not rendezvous and do not wait for other boats. Make one trip for USS LEONARD WOOD and return directly to this ship from the beach.

LCP(R)9, as soon as lowered, report to the USS FLORENCE NIGHTINGALE (PA70) to Officer of the Deck, port wing of her bridge. Return to this ship when released from beach marking duties.

LCP(R)11, as soon as lowered, report to USS LEONARD WOOD (PA12) to Officer of the Deck on port wing of bridge. Return to this ship when released from beach marking duties.

LCS(S)13, 14, report to Support Boat Division Commander at LEONARD WOOD (PA12)'s primary control vessel as soon as lowered. LCS(S)14 return to this ship immediately after assault troops have landed. LCS(S)13 remain in vicinity of yellow beach to act as traffic control boat if needed.

LCM(3)2, as soon as lowered, report to USS LEONARD WOOD (PA12) and join assembly circle on her starboard beam. Make one trip for WOOD and return directly to this ship from beach.

2400 (about) When paravanes are secured, 1st Division hoist out #5 boat and 2nd Division pick it up and set it in #15 skids. Strip all forward hatches and after half of #6 hatch. Put over all debarkation nets.

D-Day Landing Operation Orders to Ltjg. Charles S. Reder and Roscoe C. DuMond

SECRET-SECURITY

ANNEX LOVE TO COMMANDER TASK UNIT EIGHT FIVE POINT ONE POINT TWO

LANDING ATTACK ORDER 4 - 43

- -

Open fire with 50 caliber machine guns as opportunity presents itself before first wave lands.

5(e) Commence firing as above whether discovered or not.

5(h) Does not apply during this operation. Take patrol station as indicated in paragraph 5(g) above. Division Commanders permit not more than 2 boats to return at a time for refueling and rearming. When refueled and rearmed, return to patrol immediately.

6 Smoke will be employed in accordance with the doctrine set forth and as illustrated in the attached diagram.

6(a) Smoke will not be used in the Transport or Rendezvous Areas unless directed by O.T.C. or Area Commander. In general, the use of smoke at night in the vicinity of the boat lanes is not advisable and should only be undertaken in extreme urgency. The firing of smoke rockets however, on the beach in front of shore objectives is desirable.

2. GENERAL

(a) Attention is directed to Annex EASY of Commander Task Force 85 Operation Plan 4-43. Two destroyers will accompany the starboard flank of the LEONARD WOOD Assault Wave. They will commence fire at approximately the Line of Departure (where they turn off to starboard) and cease fire 6 minutes later. The pyrotechnic signal authorized for use by the first Wave Commander is as follows:

SIGNAL   MEANING

White star parachute flare   Cease Fire

(b) TBY radios will be furnished the Support Boat Squadron Commander and the Support Boat Division Commanders for use on the Boat Group Circuit. Calls as follows:

Commander LCS(S) Squadron ONE   - LCS-1
Commander LCS(S) Squad. ONE, Div. ONE - LCS-2
Commander LSC(S) Squad. ONE, Div. TWO - LCS-3

G. DRAPEAU, JR.,
Secretary   L-2

Gela, Sicily July 9, 1943, USS Harry Lee

It's 10:30 p.m. and Cooper just woke us. Says, "were in." Ensign Roscoe (DuMond) and I can't believe it but we get into our "zoot suits" tin hats, life jackets and strap on our 45s. We go top side and what a sight! We're 15,000 yards offshore and are undiscovered. Everything on the shore is ablaze and our bombers are dropping heavy stuff. Search lights are trying to pick them up and the tracers, like fingers are probing the darkness for them. The sky is filled with tracers. This is the real thing. This is war. I'm surprisingly calm.

Diary of Ltjg. Charles S. Reder

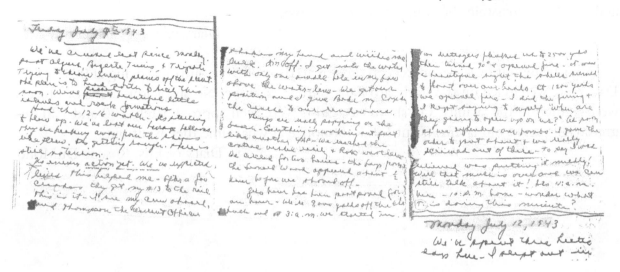

Diary of Charles S. Reder July 9–10 1943

Gela, Sicily July 10, 1943, USS Harry Lee

0000 hrs.—They have just called Roscoe and I to prepare to go over the side. Roscoe's boat is set to go first. He's loaded with 4,000 lbs. of ammunition. They pick him up with the boom then things go haywire. The steadying lines break and the 15 ton is whipped just like a feather in the breeze. His front keeps crashing against the ramps of the LCMs. I'm afraid the rockets will go off. Their fuses are set.

Diary of Ltjg. Charles S. Reder

LCS(S) Rocket Boat of Roscoe DuMond and Crew after being lowered

It took a half hour to get him to the rail. He has 2 holes in his bow. I shook his hand before he got in. The crew got aboard and they went over the side. This was wicked. He smashed up against the side of the ship. This has weakened this boat in being smashed up against the side of the ship. I'm watching over the rail and give a sigh of relief as they hit the water, slip the hook, and push away. Now it's my turn. Instead of 4 lines, I have gotten 8 steadying lines. This helped me. After a few crashes they get my number 13 to the rail. This is it. I see my crew aboard and Thompson the Warrant Officer shakes my hand and wishes me luck. I'm off. I get into the water with only a small hole in my bow, above the water line. We get our position and I give my coxswain the course to our rendezvous.

Diary of Ltjg. Charles S. Reder

After being put over, we proceeded directly to the primary control, arriving at 0045 of D-Day. Here we circled on the starboard flank of the first wave. No suspicious crafts or objects were sighted in the vicinity. On shore two lights were seen approximately 100 and 120 degrees. They were out later on, but I did not notice at what time they went out.

Diary of Ens. Roscoe DuMond

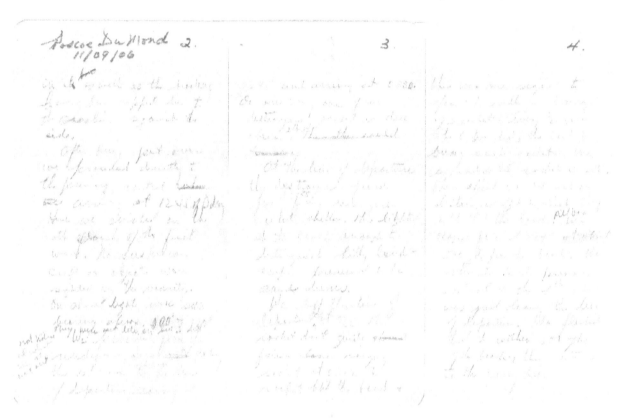

Diary of Roscoe C. DuMond July 9–10, 1943

We proceeded from the rendezvous area flanking the first wave to the line of departure, leaving at 0245 and arriving at 0330. On our way one of our destroyers passed us close abeam starboard side.

Diary of Ensign Roscoe C. DuMond

Things are really popping on the beach. Everything is working out. We reached the control vessel easily and Roscoe was there. We circled for two hours; the boys promised the USS Leonard would appear about a half hour before we shove off.

Diary of Ltjg. Charles S. Reder

Zero hour has been postponed for an hour. Were 9,000 yards off the beach and at 3 a.m. we started in. Two destroyers flanked us to 2,500 yards then turned 90% and opened fire. It was a beautiful sight. The shells seemed to float over our heads. At 1,200 yards we opened fire. I did the firing and I kept saying to myself, "when are they going to open up on us?" As soon as we expended our bombs I gave the order to put about and we really screwed out of there. To say I was relieved was putting it mildly! Well that much is over and we can still talk about it! It's 4:00 a.m. here, 10:00 p.m. home, "Wonder what (my lovely wife) is doing."

Diary of Ltjg. Charles S. Reder

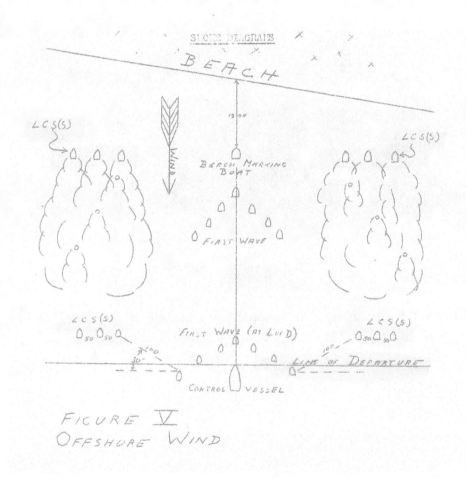

Operation Order 4–43—Support Boat Employment Plan
LCS(S) Rocket Boats to lead LCVPs, unload rockets lay smoke, then support 1st wave
At Invasion of Sicily, August 10, 1943

At the line of departure, the destroyer opened fire at 0335, firing red, green, and white shells. His lighted the beach enough to distinguish hilly landscape, presumed to be sand dunes. We left the line of departure at 0335. The rocket boat guide fired a ranging rocket at 0340. The rocket hit the beach, and this was our signal to open up with a barrage of 3 rockets approximately every half minute, which we did, the last 3 being smoke rockets. We expended 25 rockets in all. Their effect could not be distinguished, only that they all hit the beach. We ceased fire at 0345 at about 500 yards from the beach. We returned to the primary control and the 4th wave was leaving the line of departure. We flanked that to within 500 yards of the beach, and then returned to the Harry Lee. On our way back, we passed several waves proceeding to the direction of the beach. They were not our own.

Diary of Ensign Roscoe C. DuMond

LCS(S) Rocket Boats laying smoke screen at Gela, Sicily, Aug. 10, 1943, after laying Rockets, as per Operation Order 4–43. LCVPs on way in.

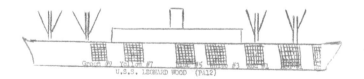

(AP Photo)

Rocket Boats

They're the Navy's LCS—land craft supporting amphibious operations. Above, they're laying a smoke-screen. They can also fire rockets.

At 1400 we were directed to the Leonard Wood. Here Commander Conlin came on board and we took him ashore to the beach master. We did not beach, but tied up alongside a pontoon from an LST. We returned to the ship at 1830. No further orders on D-Day.

Diary of Ensign Roscoe C. DuMond

SHEET # 1   INVASION OF EUROPE   GELA, SOUTH SICILY

CHARLES S. REDER
SCARSBOROUGH, NEW YORK

GELA SISILY

OUR ROCKIT BOAT OPERATION IN GELA WERE COMPLETED ON THE
FOURTEENTH OF OF JULY. THIS WAS THE FIRST COMBAT FOR THE
THE ROCKET BOATS AND IT WAS QUITE SUCCESSFUL! MY SQUADRON
SUFFERED NO DAMAGE OR LOSSES AND WE WERE HEADED BACK TO
ORAN. OUR BOATS WERE LIFTED THE HARRY E LEE TRANSPORT SHIP
AND ARRIVED AT MERS EL KABIR ON THE 16th OF JULY.

OUR SHIP STOPPED AT ORAN AND WE PUT OUR ITALIAN WOUNDED
PRISONERS ASHORE. ON JULY 18th OF JULY OUR EXECUTIVE
OFFICER INFORMED US WE WE WOULD BE TAKING 500 HUNDRED
GERMAN PRISONERS ABOARD.THEY ARE PART OF GENERAL ROMMELS
AFRICA CORPS CAPTURED BY AMERICANS IN BIZERTE ON MAY 9th
1943. I AM THE AMERICAN OFFICER IN CHARGE. I HAVE QUESTION
AND SEARCHED PRISONERS ALL AFTERNOON.GOTTEN QUITE A FEW
SOUVENIRS! THE PRISONERS ARE ALL SHORT AND STOCKY AND ARE
BLOND.SOME ARE CUTE LITTLE BASTARDS!

SCUTTLEBUT HAS IT THAT WE ARE GOING BACK TO THE STATES!
GREAT SURPRISE..AT FIVE OCLOCK A MESSENGER CAME UP ON THE
PROMENADE DECK AND TOLD ME MY BROTHER LEONARD WAS ONQUARDEC
WHAT A WONDERFUL SURPRIZE! SPENT THE NIGHT WITH ME AND HAD
SOME GOOD NAVY FOOD! LEONARD LEFT THE SHIP IN THE MORNING!
IWATCHED HIMGO DOWN THE GANGBLANK..IT LEFT A LUMP INMY THRO
WILL WE EVER SEE EACH OTHER AGAIN?

AUGUST 2nd AND WE ARE BACK STATES! GOT A THIRTY DAY LEAVE!
ROSCO AND I ARE GOING UP TO VERMOMT FOR A WEEK WITH OUR
WIVES!

WELL THE LEAVE IS OVER AND WE ARE BACK IN NORFOLK AT THE
NAVAL BASE. GOT MY ORDERS TODAY TO TAKE MY SQUADRON TO LIDO
BEACH IN LONG ISLAND,NEW YORK! WE ARE HEADED FOR EUROPE I
GUESS! I WAS RIGHT! WE LEAVE FOR SCOTLAND IN TWO DAYS!

WE ARE IN HELENSBOROUGH,SCOTLAND! I'M SURE WE ARE THE WAY
TO THE ENGLISH CHANNEL.

Charles S. Reder
10/15/2006

Sheet # 1, Invasion of Europe Gela, South Sicily

Invasion of Salerno September 3, 1943; "first documented" success of the LCS(S) Rocket Boats

Immediately after Sicily, the Invasion at Salerno, Italy began September 3th 1943. In his book U.S. Amphibious Ships and Craft published 2002, Author Norman Friedman WW2 ship expert, cites, "At Salerno the support boats proved quite useful. Initially they laid smoke to cover the landing craft from the enemy fire. The Eighth Fleet after-action report mentioned a support boat from the USS Dickman, which was covering part of the 6th Corps Green Beach. Enemy machine gun fire pinned troops of the 142nd Infantry down on the beach. The boat closed to within 80 yards on the left flank of the beach and fired salvoes of 3-4 rockets each from one flank to the other, forming a sweeping barrage of 34 rockets at a range of 750 yards. All enemy ceased fire during this attack, and when it resumed it was far weaker and directed at the LCS(S) Rocketboat, not at the troops on the beach. Later a German prisoner said that that his machine gun had been destroyed all together by rocket hits, and that his crew had been badly demoralized. The After Action report concluded that". Jerry Dause son of Ensign Leslie H. Dause stated his father talked of his Rocketboat activity there. Below is Invasion Map of Salerno.

Ensign Leslie H. Dause

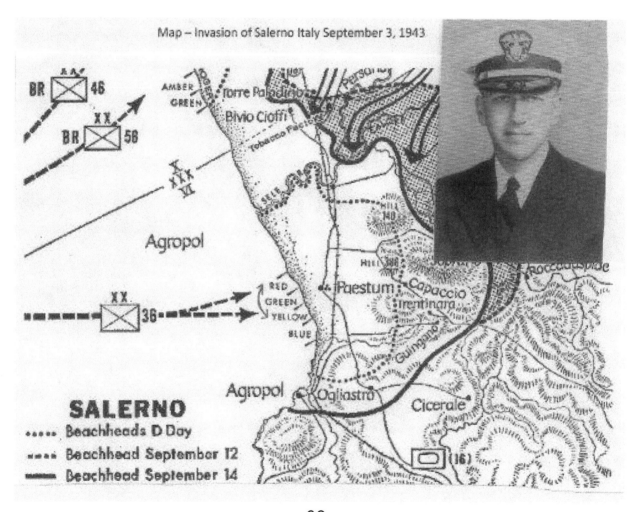

Map – Invasion of Salerno Italy September 3, 1943

CHAPTER 4

Expansion of the LCS(S)
Rocket Boat Program
in Preparation for D-Day
October 1943–February 1944

Ltjg. Charles S. Reder, Ensigns Roscoe C. DuMond & Stanley K. Jones

Expansion of the LCS(S) Rocket Boat Program
in Preparations for D-Day

Ensign Stanley K. Jones

"I was called to active duty in December 1942 and was commissioned at U.S. Navy Midshipman's School at Columbia University in New York in April 1943. When questioned as to my choice of duty, I replied, Battleship or Cruiser. I only knew that these were the largest ships. I was assigned to the U.S. Naval Amphibious Base, Little Creek, VA. for further training in small landing craft.

Ensign Stanley K. Jones

Such was the fate of many of us sailors. High expectations on large renowned ships but lost in time and records of the vast numbers of small boats.

The small boats amphibious training for large force, stealth invasions of major countries proceeded. This was successfully documented at the Invasion of Sicily in July 1943. Higgins Boats Mfg., best known for the LCVP for delivery of Invasion troops, also had large delivery orders for LCS(S) Rocket Boats. These LCS(S)s were to precede these troops with Rockets and Gunnery to clear the beaches of mines and machine gun nests.

LCS (Landing Craft Support) boats ready for delivery to the Navy

Copy of the General Plan for the LCS(S) Rocket Boat Program Expansion in anticipation of the Invasion of Europe (Normandy), given to Charles S. Reder, January 16, 1944.

FE25-5/P11

U. S. NAVAL AMPHIBIOUS TRAINING BASE
SOLOMONS, MARYLAND

16 January 1944

TRAINING OFFICER'S MEMORANDUM:

1. Commencing Monday, 17 January 1944, the Base will have 24 Rocket Boat Crews for instruction in Rockets, Smoke and Machine Guns. Each crew will consist of one officer and six men, or a total of 24 officers and 144 men.

2. Training will be under the direction of the school gunnery department. Rockets and smoke materials will be furnished by the Base to be replaced by COMPHIBTRALANT. Instruction will be held both ashore and in rocket boats afloat.

3. The Small Boats Officer is requested to have all boats in operating condition at all times for use of students.

4. Lieut. Mac Donald will arrange through the Training Officer to request replacements in rockets and smoke materials from COMPHIBTRALANT as needed.

5. Lieut. Hackett will supervise berthing and mustering of students.

6. Upon the completion of the two-week training period, a second similar group of rocket boat students will arrive for two-weeks training. Upon their graduation, a third similar group will arrive for two-weeks training; making a six-week overall rocket boat training period.

N. PHILLIPS
Commander, USN
Training Officer.

Distribution:
    Captain
    Exec. Officer
    Lieut. Frontokowski
    Lieut. Mac Donald
    Lieut. Hackett

Ltjg. Charles Simons Reder and other Officers named as Assistant Support Boat Instructors

```
                    UNITED STATES ATLANTIC FLEET
                    AMPHIBIOUS TRAINING BASE              CIS/bn

File No.
FE25-4/P16-4/00                         Little Creek, Va.
Serial No. LCT-7                        16 January 1944.



From:        The Commanding Officer.
To:          Lieutenant (jg)                          #6
             Charles REDER, D-V(G), USNR.

Subject:     Temporary duty.

Reference:   (a) ComPhibTraLant dispatch 141811 of January 1944.

      1.        In accordance with reference (a) you will proceed
immediately with Ensign Clement A. HALUPKA, D-V(G), USNR; Ensign
Maxim P. SOULIER, D-V(G), USNR; Ensign Roscoe C. DuMOND, D-V(G),
USNR; Ensign William F. BUCKLEY, D-V(G), USNR; Ensign Richard F.
O'MEARA, D-V(G), USNR; Ensign Walter W. SISSON, D-V(G), USNR; Ensign
Charles A. BURKE, D-V(G), USNR to the Amphibious Training Base,
Solomons, Maryland.  Upon arrival report to the Commanding Officer
for temporary duty as assistant support boat instructors.

      2.        This duty is in addition to your regular duties and
upon the completion thereof you will return to this command and
resume your regular duties.

      3.        Transportation via government conveyance is provided
in the execution of these orders and no commercial transportation is
authorized.

      4.        These orders are of a restricted nature and should
not be revealed to any unauthorized persons.


                                     C. F. MACKLIN, Jr.

Copy to:
   ComPhibTraLant
   C.O., ATB, Solomons, Md.
   Training Officer
```

Charles Simons Reder and his support boat instructors at Little Creek, VA, January 1944
Identified
Top row left: Ens. Richard F. Omeara
Top row center: Ensign Maxim P. Soulier
Top Row, 2nd from rt.: Ensign Clement A. Halupka
Middle row lt.: Ens. Robert A. Cannon (piggy back)
Middle row rt.: Ltjg. Charles S. Reder
Front row rt.: Ensign Roscoe C. DuMond (squatting)

Head LCS(S) Rocket Boat Training Instructor, Ltjg. Charles S. Reder

Lieutenant Junior Grade Charles Simons Reder. Born in Jersey City, NJ, July 1911. Graduated Harvard 1933: International Relations. Entered USN 1942 at Pittsfield, MA. Signed up for flight training for the Navy. Was turned down for flight training because he was red/green color blind.

Subsequently was transferred into the newly highly secret LCS "Rocket Boat" Program. Participated in First Wave of Rocket Boats at Gella in Invasion of Sicily June 1943.

Transferred back to Solomons, MD, Jan. 16, 1944. Became an Oversight Training Officer of 72 LCS(S) crews trained in 3 groups of 24 crews from Jan. 16–Feb. 28, 1944, to precede the first wave of LCVPs with rockets to knock out machine gun nests on the beaches at Omaha Beach and Utah Beach and then to flank the additional waves of LCVPs with machine gun support, smoke screens, and rockets.

On April 23, 1944 he was reassigned as Officer in Charge of Task Force K, Dispatch Boats of Force "O" off USS Ancon; Flagship of Omaha Beach. For 21 days his eight British Sea Plane Tenders ferried and hand delivered most orders and communications to the beach heads and ship to ship.

Our Flagship/Head Communications Ship; USS Ancon on D-Day—Ltjg. Charles S. Reder,

"You can observe one of our Sea Plane Tenders unloading men onto a floating dock facing opposite direction of the Ancon and Officers climbing up the side of the ladder of the flagship, returning from one of the missions to the beachhead."

Ensign Charles Roscoe Lomax
Picture provided by Ensign William H. Palmer

Copy of the First Training Group of 24 LCS(S) Rocket Boat Officers and Crews training for the Invasion of Europe (Normandy) given to Ensign Floyd Allen Ferguson, January 16, 1944. Provided by Ensign William H. Palmer

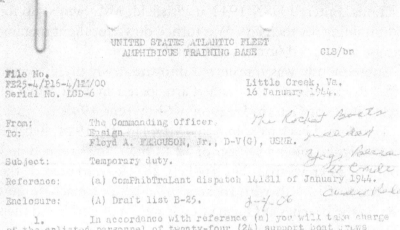

Ensign Floyd Allen Ferguson 3 Bronze Star Recipient. Normandy, Southern France, Pacific Theater
DOB: March 3, 1920
DOD: March 30, 1949
Floyd Ferguson survived the war obtaining three Bronze Stars, but tragically was killed at an early age (29) on the evening of March 31, 1949 in Mansfield, OH, when a small airplane he was flying on business crashed after hitting a telephone line on his entrance into Mansfield, OH Airport.

Even though he trained on Rocket Boats, he and 10 other officers were transferred on April 25, 1944 to Force "O" Task Force K; Dispatch Boats of the head Communications and Flag ship of Omaha Beach, the USS Ancon reporting to Ltjg. Charles S. Reder.

MANSFIELD NEWS-JOURNAL

MANSFIELDER DIES IN PLANE CRASH

Aircraft Falls On Railroad

F. A. Ferguson Jr. Dead At Willard

32

These eight British wooden sea plane tenders relayed most communications to the beachhead and other ships during the 21 days of radio silence (blackout).

He went on to serve in Southern France, probably on Rocket Boats and then the Pacific Theatre in 1945.

The Rocket Boat crews under each officer, including S2c Larry (Yogi) Berra Listed under Stoke P. Holmes (center of page)

Two weeks later, six additional crews of second group of 24 LCS(S) Rocket Boat Crews transferred to Lido Beach, NY, February 13, 1944. Document provided by Son Fred Attwood; includes the Ensign Albert M. Low crew.

```
TRAIN 13 FEBRUARY 1944
LIDO BEACH NY PFT

6 LCSS CREWS


ATTWOOD CURTIS L      ENS

SCHINDLER FRANCIS F2C      7587088
BRIDGES LEON D        S2C      8339869
PAYNE BETHEL M        S2C      8459965
HEGLIN JOHN H         F1C      8925867
ALLUMS ALBERT J JR    S1C      6048677
ASCHTGEN DONALD L     F2C      7267265
                           6

SMITH GEORGE F        ENS

COOKE JAMES T         S2C      8353927
BARKER DELBERT F      S2C      8953005
STEFFY JOSEPH J       S2C      8186891
DIXON JOHN C          F1C      6226701
KEENAN FRANKLIN J     S1C      5175590
EWING FLOYD E JR      F2C      8765538
                           6

LOW ALBERT M          ENS

MC CANDLESS C G JR    F1 MOM8221456
BERGAMO JERRY J       S2C      8155316
REW CHARLES R JR      MOMM3C6055887
DOLAN THOMAS J        S2C      8119028
BIRCH CLINTON E       S2C      6674089
FORD WILLIAM L        S1C      6092425
                           6

DAILY JAMES L         ENS

ANGEL LEE O           S1C      6339409
RASMUSSEN HERBERT     F1 MOM8525178
DELLINDIA JOHN A      F2 MOM7109885
ELLISON ROY           S2C      6135211
BARROWS HENRY R       S2C      8008869
ARCHIBALD W B JR      S2C      8306725
                           6

DESMOND FRANCIS J     ENS

PAICH RUDOLPH         COX      8225635
DEPPE ROBERT W        S2C      2497579
NORRIS CHARLES J      S2C      8952166
RISCHENOLE SAMUEL J   S2C      8060375
O MALLEY WILLIAM F    F2 MOM8576983
GHYZEL KENNETH W      MOMM3C8053944
                           6

HURLEY STUART P       ENS

HAMMETT ARTHUR C      S2C      8052996
GUERINI JOSEPH F      S2C      8581140
HAWKINS PAUL E        S2C      8952991
BACH ROBERT F         F2C      7111481
BEAVERS JESSE G       S2C      8356920
FUKA EMIL J           F2C      8765238
```

Original 24 Rocket Boat Officers for D-Day

Utah Beach
Ens. Lemuel C. Laney

Omaha Beach
Ens. Curtis L. Attwood

Utah Beach
Ens. Stoke P. Holmes

Utah Beach
Ens. Ralph E. Frede

Utah Beach
Southern France
Ens. Albert M. Low

Sicily
Utah Beach/Southern France
Ens. Robert Goldsmith

Commendation - Utah Beach
Purple Heart/Silver Star -
Southern France

Omaha Beach
Southern France
Ens. Herman F. Vorel

Omaha Beach
Southern France
Ltjg. Nicholas J. Zuras

Omaha Beach
Southern France
Ens. Edwin H. Lemkin

Omaha Beach
Southern France
Ens. Peter J. Lojko

Omaha Beach
Ens. Elmer "Chick" J. Oist

Omaha Beach
Ens. Robert A. Cannon

•Commendation -
Southern France

D-Day LST 355
Ens. Paul H. Zent

D-Day LST 307
LSM(R) - Invasion of Japan
Ens. Harry W. Tennant

D-Day - LST/LCVP
Southern France
Ens. Leslie H. Dause

D-Day - Dispatch Boats
Force "O"
Southern France
Ens. Floyd A. Ferguson

D-Day - Dispatch Boats
Force "O"
Southern France
Ens. Albert B. Cranwell

D-Day - Dispatch Boats
Force "O"
Southern France
Ens. Frank J. Desmond

D-Day Dispatch Boats
Force "O"
Ens. Maxim Paul Soulier

D-Day Dispatch Boats
Force "O"
Ens. William J. Martin

D-Day Dispatch Boats
Force "O"
Ens. William H. Palmer

D-Day Dispatch Boats
Force "O"
Ens. Abner T. Winslow

D-Day Dispatch Boats
Force "O"
Ens. Daniel H. Ridder

D-Day Dispatch Boats
Force "O"
Ens. Carl Van Bennett

**Expansion of the LCS(S) Rocket Boat Program
in Preparation for D-Day**

Two Weeks Daily Rocket Boat Training Schedule for Training Officer Charles S. Reder

U. S. NAVAL AMPHIBIOUS TRAINING BASE
SOLOMONS, MARYLAND

ROCKET BOAT (LCS(S)) TRAINING SCHEDULE

Day	Group A	Group B	Group C	Class
1st	Small Arms	30 Cal. Mach. Gun	Loading Drill and Signalling	P.M. Only
2nd	30 Cal. M.G. / 50 Cal. M.G.	50 Cal. Mach. Gun / Bolt Cart.	Tactical Maneuvers / Tactical Maneuvers and Dry Runs	A.M. / P.M.
3rd	Gas Masks / Repeat Small Arms Plus Cable Cutter	Firing 30&50 Cal. Machine Gun / Clean Guns & Loading Drill and S.B. Signals	30 Cal. Mach. Gun / 50 Cal. Mach. Gun	A.M. / P.M.
4th	Bolt Cart. / Fire 30&50 Cal. Mach. Gun	Tactical Maneuvers / Gas Masks	Gas Masks / Bolt Cart.	A.M. / P.M.
5th	Load. Drill S.B. Signals / Tactical Maneuvers	Small Arms / Cable Cutter & Small Arms	Fire 30&50 Cal. MG / Clean M.G. Plus Loading Drill and Signals	A.M. / P.M.
6th	Tactical Maneuvers / Loading Drill and Signals	Loading Drill and Signals / Tactical Maneuvers	Small Arms / Cable Cutters and Small Arms	A.M. / P.M.
7th	Rockets-- Smoke Pots / Instruction in Maneuvers	Rockets-- Smoke Pots / Instruction in Maneuvers	Loading Drill / Signal and Tactical Mnvrs.	A.M. / P.M.
8th	Fire Rockets Lay Smoke / Mach. Guns & Small Arms	Mach. Guns & Small Arms / Fire Rockets Lay Smoke	Rockets-- Smoke Pots / Instruction in Maneuvers	A.M. / P.M.
9th	Load. Drill Sig. Tactiqvr. / Fire Rockets Lay Smoke	Small Arms / Educational Movie	Fire Rockets Lay Smoke / Machine Guns & Small Arms	A.M. / P.M.
10th	Small Arms / Educational Movie	Fire Rockets Lay Smoke / Loading Drill Signals Tactical Maneuvers	Educational Movie / Fire Rockets Lay Smoke	A.M. / P.M.
11th	TACTICAL MANEUVERS BY ENTIRE FLOTILLA			A.M.

Lt(jg) Charles S. REDER
Officer in Charge of LCS(S) Training

Ensign Albert B. Cranwell at helm with crew in maneuvers at Solomons, MD, January 1944
Front view of bridge with twin 50s.

Ensign Richard F. O'Meara at helm of LCS(S) Rocket boat in Maneuvers. Solomons, MD, January 1944

Ensign Albert B. Cranwell's crew
Rear view of bridge with two 30s.

Expansion of the LCS(S) Rocket Boat Program
in preparations for D-Day

Rocket Boat Training Certificate Issued to Gunner; George H. Hartley
of Ensign albert B. Cranwells Crew
issued from Little Creek Va.
ending official Rocket Boat Training in the States

AMPHIBIOUS FORCE
LANDING CRAFT
UNITED STATES ATLANTIC FLEET

This is to certify that_____
has successfully completed the courses prescribed for
training in attack boats.

Notation to this effect is hereby authorized to be placed on the in-
dividual's record by his commanding officer.

DATE JAN 16 1944

ATTACK BOAT COMMANDER

C. F. MACKLIN, JR.
CAPTAIN, U. S. NAVY
COMMANDING OFFICER

C. F. Macklin Jr.

Gunner George Harold Hartley

Next stop for the Rocket Boat Crews was Lido Beach Long Island for 2 weeks Feb 1, 1944-Feb. 15, 1944 then 6 week transport to England Via LST convoys across the Atlantic.

Transfer Orders to Officer in Charge Robert H. Goldsmith
for 25 Rocket Boat Crews to Lido Beach Long Island, January 31, 1944

UNITED STATES ATLANTIC FLEET
File No.   AMPHIBIOUS TRAINING BASE   CLS/hk
FE25-4/P16-4/MM/00
Serial NO. LCD-152   Little Creek, Va.
R-E-S-T-R-I-C-T-E-D   31 January 1944.

From: The Commanding Officer.
To: Ensign
             Robert H. GOLDSMITH, D-V(G), USNR.

Subject: Change of duty.

Reference: (a) ComPhibTraLant Speedletter FE25/P16-3/00/MM
                 Serial 0042 of 23 January 1944.
             (b) BuPers ltr. Pers-312-VM of 20 December 1943.

Enclosure: (A) Draft list A-87.

   1.   In accordance with references (a) and (b) the
following are hereby detached from their present duty with the
Amphibious Training Command, U.S. Atlantic Fleet, and any other such
duties as may have been assigned them, and when directed, Ensign
Robert H. GOLDSMITH, D-V(G), USNR will take charge of one hundred
and fifty (150) enlisted personnel as listed in enclosure (A); will
proceed immediately with Ensign Ralph E. FREDE, D-V(G), USNR; Ensign
Leslie H. DAUSE, D-V(G), USNR; Ensign Carl V. BENNETT, D-V(G), USNR;
Ensign Floyd A. FERGUSON, Jr., D-V(G), USNR; Ensign Peter J. LOJKO,
D-V(G), USNR; Ensign Morris GLRBLR, D-V(G), USNR; Ensign Albert B.
CRANWELL, Jr., D-V(G), USNR; Ensign Lemuel C. LANEY, D-V(G), USNR;
Ensign Paul H. ZENT, D-V(G), USNR; Ensign William H. PALMER, D-V(G),
USNR; Ensign William J. MARTIN, Jr., D-V(G), USNR; Ensign Daniel H.
RIDDER, D-V(G), USNR; Ensign Nicholas J. ZURAS, D-V(G), USNR; Ensign
Abraham M. NATHAN, D-V(G), USNR; Ensign Edwin H. LEMKIN, D-V(G),
USNR; Ensign Abner T. WINSLOW, D-V(G), USNR; Ensign Stoke P. HOLMES,
D-V(G), USNR; Ensign Harry W. TENNANT, D-V(G), USNR; Ensign Robert
A. CANNON, D-V(G), USNR; Ensign F. E. CRAWFORD, Jr., D-V(G), USNR;
Ensign Herman F. VOREL, D-V(G), USNR; Ensign Maxim P. SOULIER,
D-V(G), USNR; Ensign Clement A. HALUPKA, D-V(G), USNR; Lieutenant
(jg) Charles S. REDER, D-V(G), USNR to the Advance Base Assembly
and Training Unit, Naval Training Center, Lido Beach, Long Island,
New York. Upon arrival, you will report to the Commanding Officer
for further transfer in accordance with reference (a).

   2.   The Disbursing Officer, Receiving Station, N.O.B.,
Norfolk, Virginia is authorized and requested to furnish the
necessary transportation, subsistence and baggage transfers for the
proper execution of these orders.

   3.   The records and accounts of the men in your charge
are handed you herewith for safe delivery to your new Commanding
Officer.

   4.   These orders are of a restricted nature and should
not be divulged to any unauthorized persons.

                                        C. F. MACKLIN, JR.

Copy to:
  BuPers
  ComPhibTraLant
  ComTHREE
  ComFIVE

Ens. Robert H. Goldsmith

Rocket Boat Missions at Sicily, July 1943; Utah Beach, June 6, 1944; and Southern France, August 15, 1944. Training oversight Rocket Boat Officer, January 16–31, 1944

Sailing Orders to Rocket Boat Officers After Two Weeks
at Lido Beach Long Island to Cross the Atlantic

The first group that completed training left February 18, 1944; the next, on March 7; the last on March 21

Top Row Ensigns:
Robert H. Goldsmith
Robert A. Cannon
Stoke P. Holmes

Bottom Row Ensigns:
Frank E. Crawford
Maxim Soulier

Ensigns:
William J. Martin
Stoke P. Holmes
Frank E. Crawford
Clement A. Halupka
Maxim Soulier

CHAPTER 5

Crossing the Atlantic
via LST Convoys
February 18, 1944–April 4, 1944

Ensign Albert M. Low, Gunner Yngvar Tjersland,

MoMMs Jess Delgadilla & Walter V. Varnum, Seaman Yogi Berra

Crossing the Atlantic February 18, 1944–April 4, 1944

25 Rocket Boat Crews depart on different LSTs on Trans Atlantic Convoy

After training we were sent as a group to New York, where we and our new rocket boats were loaded aboard the LST 51. They were placed on the deck of an LCT that was in turn placed on the main deck of the LST. From there the ship went to Boston, then as the convoy formed up left the U.S. and headed for Halifax, NS, we learned early on, the LST was not a stable platform to sail on. Word was that it would rock in a bathtub, which it much resembled. As this was the 15th of February, the weather and seas were not to be trifled with; we could not see the other ships in the convoy when in a wave trough, the sea spray would freeze on the gun tubs we were assigned to as lookouts, 30 days of freezing and upchucking brought us to Glasgow, Scotland and even a short liberty, then to Plymouth, England, where the Rocket boats were taken off by crane and the LCT slid off by tilting the LST. Walter V. Varnum, Motormac

From the Amphibious Base at Solomons, MD, we went to the Brooklyn Navy Yard. There we embarked on the LST 53.

Officers might serve on battleships or cruisers for half a career without drawing duty on the bridge. But I, an ensign, stood the JOOD (Junior Officer on Deck) watch during my first night at sea.

LSTs on Convoy to England
Picture provided by Ensign Robert Cannon

Midnight to 0400 watches tend to be spooky, but knowing that the coastal corridor was a hunting area for German subs, my imagination bloomed. I pictured submarines lurking in the ocean's rollers and saw torpedo trails in the foam streams. The captain and OODs must have been nervous too, as general quarters sounded with disturbing regularity. After being subjected to so many alarms that a full night's sleep seemed unnatural, we made it to Halifax, Nova Scotia, where we stood by for a few days.

While there, I took possession of a rocket boat so new that the engine registered zero hours. A plaque on the firing box advertised, "Designed and Mfg. at M.I.T." Gunner's Mate MacAndrews and I took an entire day to check the racks for parallax, recalibrate, and attach firing circuits. After a thorough check, the boat was covered with a tarpaulin. As were our orders, it was classified Top Secret.

Ensigns Nick Zuras and Herman Vorel with binoculars on LST 282
on JOOD watch crossing the Atlantic, March 1944

From there, we took position in a convoy for a forty day transit to Pembroke Dock, Wales, Great Britain. The convoy was escorted by fast charging corvettes, smaller than destroyers, but more agile. Their sonar emitted pinging sounds which experienced listeners could translate to know where to charge after unseen submarines. Our very large convoy had a screen of only four corvettes which were expert at warding off submersibles, and sometimes even destroying them. However, if only one were lured from its position, subs might enjoy a turkey shoot at our convoy's expense.

We passed ships that had lost their way. They projected a sense of helplessness few would ever know. They might hope for survival by way of a miracle, but there were few miracles beyond the protection of the British corvettes. With the onset of darkness came explosions and fires. Thank God we couldn't hear the cries.

Ensign Albert M. Low

American Submarine Chaser/Royal Navy called them corvettes

The trip over the Atlantic to Glasgow, Scotland on an LST, I could remember many sailors were on it but most of them were sick. It was awful. You would lie in your bunk and think what would happen if you hit a mine or were hit by a torpedo. The bulkhead would cave in, and you knew you couldn't swim. We were cannon fodder. I can now understand why old men send young men to war.

Yogi Berra, Seaman 2c

Our LST492 included Yogi Berra. We left Halifax, Nova Scotia and landed at Milford Haven Whales, England. We encountered two submarines attacks. Our escort sunk two. Yngvar Ttjersland, Gunner

Convoy of 80 ships

German subs torpedoed 2 tankers

When I left for Boston, we went to Halifax, Nova Scotia and sailed for Europe March 5, 1944 with a convoy of 80 ships. The Canadian Navy shepherded us for two days then went back. On the third night the German subs torpedoed two tail tankers. The sky all lit up in on the horizon.

Jess Delgadilla, Motormac

All three LST convoys, including 432 Rocketmen, arrived at various Southern England Advanced Amphibious Training Bases between March 26–April 15, 1944. They continued Rocket Boat training maneuvers until D-Day.

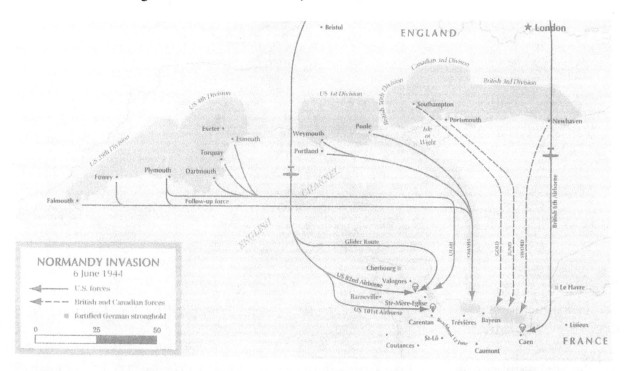

Upon arrival in England and the determination that only 24 of the original 72 LCS(S) Crews were necessary for Normandy, most of the original LCS(S) Rocket Boat Crews and Officers were transferred to fill other gaps for D-Day.

Rocket Boat crew members transferred to other duties for D-Day

Ensign Morris Gerbers LCS(S) Crew
Leroy Graham, Motormac
Henry Lovelace, Seaman 2c
Yngvar Tjersland, Gunner

Our LCS(S) Rocket Boat idling in Salerno, Italy August 1944 with our whole crew aboard. Additional members of crew not in picture, to left, Joseph Loiodice S1c, Ray Lojewski, S2c Rex Wachs, Motormac.

The final number of Rocket Boat Crews that were used for D-Day was 24; 12 at Omaha, 12 at Utah; as per Ensign Ralph E. Frede's D-Day LCS(S) Summary.

This left a surplus of 48 Rocket Boat Crews who were fully trained for small boat amphibious duties to be deployed in other duties for D-Day.

Top picture provided by Yngvar Tjersland, who was transferred to LST 157 for D-Day and participated in the Invasion.

Joseph Onischuck, left, from Ensign Frank E. Crawford's crew, stayed in England on D-Day doing communications work. Louis Roberti, right, transferred to LST 51 for D-Day circa May 1, 1944

CHAPTER 6

Arrival at England's Advanced Amhibious Training Bases
March 26, 1944–April 20, 1944

Ensigns Stanley Kenneth Jones & William H. Palmer,
Coxswain Mario Preato, Motormac Walter Varnum

Ensign William H. Palmer

Ensign William H. Palmer's Rocket Boat Crew # 7 at St. Mawes, Cornwall, England, March 17, 1944

Carl Whitaker, Charles J. Watson, Gunner Mario Preato, Coxswain Dominic Vittorio, James Spina, Motormac John Sindlinger

Arrival in England

"Upon arrival in St. Mawes, Cornwall, England, 6 of the Ensigns and crews had the use of six homes."

Mario Preato, Coxswain

Clarification: Living quarters at St. Mawes
The crews and the new boats were all sent to St. Mawes a small village to the south of England. We were quartered in a doctor's house that was said to be one of the better homes in the town, no running water or bathrooms inside, each room had a single light bulb and a small fireplace, we had jury rigged showers (cold) outside, but after our initiation into the great seas it seemed like Paradise, we spent the time getting used to our boats and practicing maneuvers and marching around the country side. One of the unusual features of this area was the huge tides 30 to 40 feet so you had to plan how to get from one side of the bay to the other.

Walter Varnum, MoMM3c

Our House—Pictures provided by Walter Varnum MoMM3c
circled house occupied by Walter Varnum and Rocket Boat crew in St. Mawes

"St. Mawes was a sleepy little village across the bay from Falmouth, surrounded by several barrage balloons and inhabited by friendly warm people. We had only been there a few hours until "Jerry" (German Planes) flew over to give us a look. Sirens went off, the balloons activated but no bombs were dropped. The native population said they (the [Jerries]) just wanted us to know they knew we where over there."

Ensign Stanley Kenneth Jones

Picture of all Officers in my group upon arrival at St. Mawes England
Ensign Stanley Kenneth Jones

Picture of Ensigns provided by Ensign Stanley K. Jones
Top row, 4th from left: Ens. Charles Roscoe Lomax; 2nd row down, 2nd from left: Ens. William Howard Palmer; 2nd row down, 6th from left: Ens. Stanley Kenneth Jones; bottom row, 4th from right: Lt. Moses; top row, 5th from left: Ens. Franklin A. Fleece; top row, 2nd from right: Ens. Floyd A. Ferguson

Other Pictures of Crew Members Identified and Unidentified
Identified by John H. Schmitt and Walter Varnum
Taken behind barbed wire fence; playing field enclosure, Salerno, Italy

L/R Top Row: James Houde LCS(S) Rocket Boat under Ensign Goldsmith on U.S.S. Bayfield on D-Day, Ed Lanier; ST1547, Anthony Russo; ST1626, James Spina; ST1627 Robert Myers; ST1626, Joe Johnson; ST320, Walter Varnum; ST1546
L/R Bottom: John Schmitt; ST1546, Frank Ravnikar; ST1549, Leroy Cassort; ST1549, Unknown, John Muccina, ST1586

After another 6 weeks of Rocket Boat Training, 24 Rocket Boat Crews loaded onto various APA, Attack Transports, and LSTs, such as USS Bayfield, U.S.S. Dickman, U.S.S. Barnett, U.S.S. Samuel Chase, and crossed the English Channel late night, early morning, June 5, 6, and arrived off Utah Beach, Omaha Beach at 2:00 a.m. and started unloading.

This map shows all Ports of exit and routes to Omaha and Utah beaches, June 5 & 6, 1944

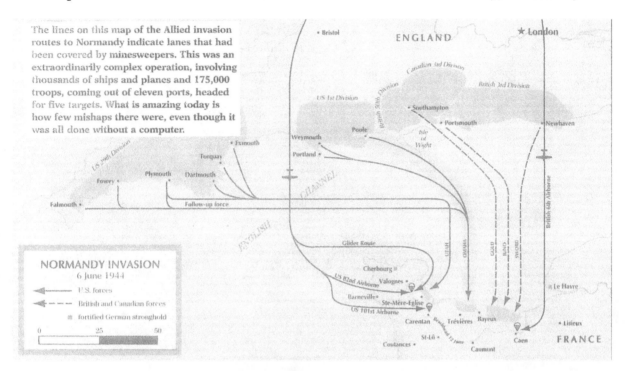

The lines on this map of the Allied invasion routes to Normandy indicate lanes that had been covered by minesweepers. This was an extraordinarily complex operation, involving thousands of ships and planes and 175,000 troops, coming out of eleven ports, headed for five targets. What is amazing today is how few mishaps there were, even though it was all done without a computer.

One last look at Teignmouth; Devon; England Picture provided by Ensign Herman F. Vorel

55

CHAPTER 7

D-Day Operation Overlord at Utah Beach
Northern France
June 6, 1944

Ensigns Ralph E. Frede, Lemuel C. Laney, Albert M. Low & Stuart P. Hurley,
Gunner Albert W. Coogan, Seamen Harry M. Fleisher, James J. Houde & Yogi Berra

Here is one of the first pictures of the U.S. Navy rocket ship. Known as an **LCS (landing craft, support)**, the new ship carries machine-guns and also rocket racks amidships. It was used in the **Normandy Landings**, the Navy revealed recently, a Navy communications section demonstrates it, with the rocket explosion shown in inset. U.S. Navy Photo. LCS Rocket Boat picture provided by Seaman 1c Harry M. Fleisher

Utah Beach
Ensign Ralph E. Frede

A proud Texan was Ralph E. Frede. Born September 28, 1921 in Floyada, Texas. He graduated from Baylor College of Medicine with a degree in Journalism. He later obtained a Master's Degree in Government and went on to become Vice President of Public Affairs at Baylor College of Medicine. He was married to Mary Chambers on December 25, 1946. They had five children; daughters. He consolidated and donated his LCS(S) Rocket Boat Mission highlights to the University of Texas in Austin on April 28, 1998. Even though this is the shortest of summaries in words, it lays the basic parameters of the LCS(S) Rocket Boat Plan at Utah and Omaha beaches. Ralph passed away on January 1, 2005.

Ensign Ralph E. Frede

Highlights of Ensign Ralph E. Frede's D-Day LCS(S) Rocket Boat Mission from his presentation on the next few pages.

(1) Reviewed (attached) Invasion map of Utah Beach, June 4, 1944

(2) Crossed the English Channel on USS Barnet APA 5

(3) Disembarked from the USS Barnet; APA 5 at 2 a.m. June 6, 1944

(4) 24 LCS(S) Rocket Boats in total: 12 for Utah Beach, 12 for Omaha

(5) Finding the control boat

(6) All forming a line parallel to the beach

(7) Proceeding in at 6:08 a.m. into Utah Beach Red and Green, while being shelled at by Bofors 88's

(8) Problem keeping men down and out of the line of fire

(9) Control boat is sunk: floated out of position

(10) Fire rockets and machine guns about 6:00 a.m.

(11) LCS(S) Rocket Boat sunk in big storm two weeks after invasion off Omaha Beach

USS Barnett

Utah Beach—Rocket Boat Invasion Map utilized by Ens. Ralph E. Frede LCS(S)
Rocket Boat Crew on June 4, 1944

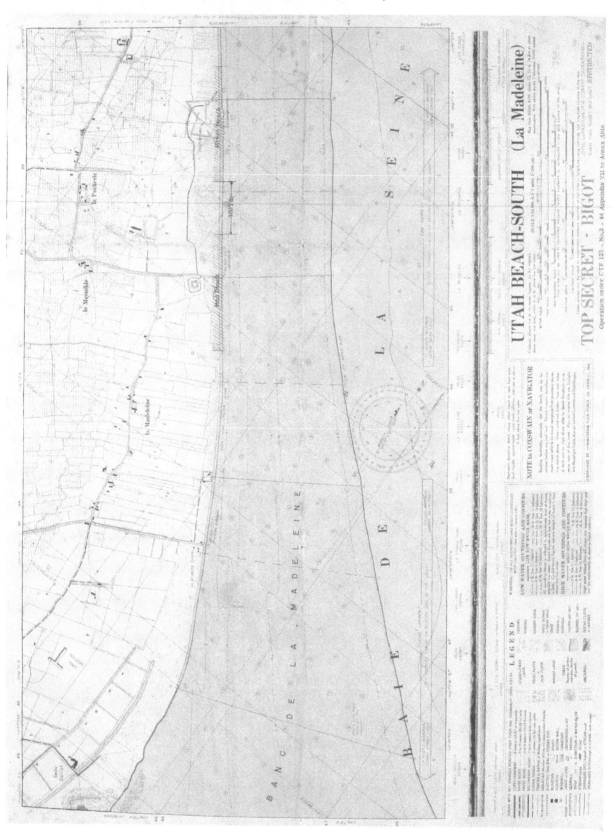

Ensign Ralph E. Frede
His actual self-edited summary of highlights of speech given April 28, 1944; page 1

One Naval Officer's View of World War II

LAMP presentation: 1:00 p.m., April 28, 1998

Slide 8 Acknowledge Ed Fisher's contribution and participation
        E. O. Box for slides

Sunday morning - Dec. 6, 1941 - APO meeting, Texas Union, *U.T. campus*

January, '42 - V-7   *Spring '43*
    editor, DAILY TEXAN

Midshipman School, Northwestern U., Chicago campus
    10th floor of Abbott Hall overlooking Lake Michigan

Navy Pier - 28th Ocotber - Commissioned Ensign, USNR

1.
Amphibious duty in Little Creek, VA to Feb., '44
    Personal view of Chicago, New York, Norfolk
    LCVP - LCM, LCT, ~~LCS~~ Hadn't heard of an LCS(S)

    But in Feb. '44 got LCS(s) Training

    Tell about an LCS(S) - 48 rockets - w twin 50 caliber machine gun
        Ensign and 6 ~~enlisted~~ men on crew

LCI to Providence, New York   Lido Beach

#2
2.
LST 491 to Halifax, Nova Scotia   *(LST 743 - Ed's ship shown)*
    Winter convoy to Plymouth, England *&*   *in slide*
    Zig zagging across the Atlantic in winer
    4 on and 4 off for two weeks - *Canadian corvettes*
    Arrived Plymouth: 18 March, 1944

Fowey in Cornwall, Milford Haven, *Wales*
Dartmouth - Royal Naval College
    air raids and fox-holes

3.
Practice invasion - Lyme Bay (Slapton Sands) 27 and 28 April
    German E Boats sank three LSTs - 749 men died. *"Devon Coast disaster"*

4.
USS Barnett - APA 5 - Loch Long, Scotland
    (the Scottish people)
Invasion of Normandy

    Briefing two nights before (June 4)
    What we were told about casualities
        One officer's reaction
        Map of the invasion beach - Utah
        June 5 - Barnett to our position
        The Battleship Texas - *16 inch shells*

    One night before invasion

June 6 - PUt in water at 2:00 a.m. - the trip to Utah Beach
        24 of our boats - 12 on Utah and 12 on Omaha
        Seeing the Control Boat - forming a line parallel
            to the beach. ~~Before~~
        Bofors 88's hitting in Water - problem to keep men down.

Ensign Ralph E. Frede
His actual self-edited summary of highlights of speech given April 28, 1944; page 2

page 2 - World War II

5. Control Boat sunk: floated out of position
   Fired rockets and machine gun - about 6:00 a.m.

6. Picked up dead sailor and back to Barnett
   HOLD UP UTAH MAP -
   What was it like?   Pretty damned exciting!
      (describe scene)
                       barrage baloons - anti =aircraft fire
   HMS CERES for about 2 weeks ~ E. G. - *Looking for a mine*

   ~~DUKW~~ several days after invasion ASHORE :

   ~~DUKW~~   Colonel directing traffic

   DUKW pulls out of water : Eisenhower, Montgomery, ADm. King
                             Powell - the entire top command
                                      staff

   Activities while aboard HMS Ceres

      ~~Search for axi   floating mine~~
      Storm :   my boats sunk off Omaha Beach
      Survivors back to Plymouth

Ensigns Lemuel Laney and Stokes P. Holmes
S2c Larry (Yogi) Berra under Ens. Stoke P. Holmes

Ensign Lemuel C. Laney

Lemuel C. Laney was born June 19, 1918 in Maiden, NC. He graduated North Carolina State University with honors, majoring in Animal Husbandry/Science. He became County Agricultural Extension Agent, 31 years in his home county. He was married to Elizabeth Jordan on August 6, 1946, and had five children. As of the publication of this book, he still resides in North Carolina.

Ensign Stoke P. Holmes

Stoke P. Holmes was born September 24, 1921. He graduated from the Texas College of Arts & Industries, majoring in Math and Physics. He became a district sales manager for Exxon Oil. He married Sarah Marie Kullen on November 15, 1942. They had one son and one daughter. Stoke passed away on June 16, 2001. He was Yogi Berra's commanding officer from January 1944 through D-Day until June 27th 1944.

Ensigns Lemuel C. Laney and Stoke P. Holmes both were transported across the English Channel on June 5, 6 on Coast Guard Transport USS Bayfield. S2c Larry (Yogi) Berra was under Stoke P. Holmes. Disembarking from the USS Bayfield at 2:00 a.m., June 6, 1944, they rode their LCS(S) Rocket Boats into Utah Beach across from each other. Lemuel Laney has written their summary on the following pages.

USS Bayfield, PA33, Coastguard

Rocket Boat Setup Men

Gunner; Robert A. York

I'm Robert A. York, a gunners mate that was aboard the USS Bayfield. I, along with gunners mate Walter Conjura, were in charge of the rocket department. The day before the Normandy Invasion we worked to the early morning installing the detonators on the rockets and put 24 in each rack so they could be hoisted aboard the rocket boats early in the morning of June 6, 1944. We had 4 LCS(S) Rocket Boats. The boats were lowered first then the rockets and then secured in place. These boats were to lead our LCVPs.

What follows on the next page is our list of Rocket Boat Officers and Crews on the USS Bayfield on D-Day June 6th 1944 which I kept. Following this list is Ensign Lemuel Laney's account of his Rocket Boat Mission on D-Day.

Utah Beach
Ensigns Lemuel Laney; Stokes P. Holmes
S2c Larry (Yogi) Berra under Ens. Stoke P. Holmes

The following June 6th roster of the USS Bayfield shows 5 Rocket Boat Officers from the Navy that worked off the USS Bayfield on D-Day. Ensigns Laney and Holmes are listed 4 and 5, while Yogi Berra is listed just below in the Navy Boat Enlisted Men. He is listed 5th. All yellow highlighted are identified original LCS(S) Rocket Boat Crews who trained January 16, 1944–January 31, 1944 in Solomons, MD.

Rocket Boat Crews 1,2,3 noted the original crews that trained together in Solomons, MD, Jan. 1944

No.	NAME	SERIAL No.	RANK OR RATE AS OF END OF MONTH	REMARKS
	...of the Officers and Crew of the U. S. Coast Guard	USS BAYFIELD (APA-31)		for the month of _____
1.	GOLDSMITH, Robert H.	—	Lieut(jg)	1337,8—Tr to the USS ROBERTSON for duty. AUTH: CO USS BAYFIELD/L 8 June '44 (APA33/CO-73-781-201
2.	KERZLORN, Alfred H.	188550	Lieut(jg)	do
3.	RYKACZEWSKI, Aloisius F.	—	Lieut(jg)	do
4.	HOLMES, Stoke P.	—	Ensign	do
5.	LANEY, Lemuel G.	—	Ensign	do
	NAVY BOAT ENLISTED MEN TRANSFERRED			
1.	ADAMS, Alfred, Jr.	244 80 45	S1c	1337,8—Tr to the USS ROBERTSON AUTH: CO USS BAYFIELD/L 8 June
2.	ANDERSON, Paul J.	810 18 22	SM3c	do
3.	BANKES, Roland A.	244 67 76	Cox.	do
4.	BERGER, Joseph J.	238 89 78	Sea2c	do
5.	BERRA, Lawrence P.	835 99 55	S2c	do
6.	BOUDREAU, Edward A.	825 33 27	S2c	do
7.	CLARKSON, Lewis S.	722 60 72	S1c	do
8.	CONWAY, Charles	245 39 33	S1c	do
9.	COOGAN, Albert W.	862 46 15	F2c	do
10.	COULTER, George H.	609 91 22	LoM3c	do
11.	DE STEFANO, Anthony F.	711 58 97	S2c	do
12.	DUNHAM, John A.	7 1 17 16	MoM3c	do
13.	FLEISHER, Harry M.	249 88 56	S1c	do
14.	FRENCH, Howard O.	337 11 00	BM1c	do
15.	GIRASULO, Eugene A.	807 53 46	S2c	do
16.	GLUECKERT, Wilmer W.	612 83 56	S1c	do
17.	GREENFIELD, Sam (n)	284 63 35	MoM2c	...TSON of duty. AUTH:CO BAYFIELD/L 8 June,'44 (APA33/CO-73-283-201
18.	HALL, Robert E.	347 10 81	MoM3c	do
19.	HIRT, Jack F.	321 80 07	MoM2c	do
20.	HOUDE, James J.	807 53 50	S2c	do
21.	KINCADE, Arley D.	563 39 95	MoM1c	do
22.	LEITCH, William L.	256 44 39	SM2c	do
23.	LEVESQUE, Irenee P.	573 05 77	MoM2c	do
24.	MASSARO, Thomas (n)	608 79 41	SM3c	do
25.	MOORE, Howard J.	708 42 93	S1c	do
26.	MULIVICH, Michael G.	805 91 70	S2c	do
27.	POULOS, George D.	628 26 33	F2c	Do
28.	RAILEY, John C.	657 02 04	Cox.	*Excellent* do
29.	ROGREN, Peter W.	376 91 59	MoM1c	do
30.	ROUTEN, Harschel D.	669 85 91	BM2c	do
31.	SCHWARZ, Clarence R.	633 36 55	MoM3c	do
32.	SMITH, Wilson	575 89 18	S2c	*stop on Lordy K.H.del*
33.	STANDERT, Walter	245 57 54	S1c	do
34.	STEWART, Robert A.	208 98 36	GM3c	do
35.	STRATTON, Jason E.	835 65 44	S2c	do
36.	SULLIVAN, Harold H.	813 95 36	S2c	do
37.	TABLER, Richard E.	224 74 89	F1c	do
38.	TRAFTON, Allan C.	2 3 99 14	S1c	do
39.	VAN EPP, Corwin H., Jr.	268 75 85	BM1c	do
40.	WINNINGHAM, Joseph M.	605 62 29	S2c	do

Actual Summary of Ensign Lemuel C. Laney of his Rocket Boat mission at Utah Beach D-Day Ensign with Stoke P. Holmes (Yogi Berra's Crew)

While we were aboard the Bayfield, we went out one dark night for landing craft practice to hit a beach somewhere in the English Channel. My boat and crew were dropped overboard and told to take a certain degree course and head for the beach. We hit the water fine, but of course my boat would not start. It wouldn't start and it was a dark night with not a light anywhere and we started drifting. We drifted away from the ship. We had no idea how far or what direction. But finally we got the motor started after about 30 minutes. We talked about what direction to take, nobody knew, me and my four crew members. I said let's try such and such direction. We started and went in that direction, and the Lord was with us I guess, because we hit the beach exactly where we were supposed to be, but we were at least a half an hour late.

Back aboard the APA 33 Bayfield, we were dropped off again about midnight. This was for the invasion, but I'm not sure whether we were told that we were headed for the invasion or not. I guess we were. We were to start our motor, start out in such and such a degree, go to the beach, I forgot the distance, probably 300 to 400 feet from the beach, and fire our rockets. The ship anchored about nine miles from the shore, so we had about nine miles to go in the dark. It was dark then, later daylight. About daylight or getting daylight by the time we got near the shore to fire our rockets. We were at Utah Beach.

We were going in a wave with some other rocket boats. How many were in the wave, I am not sure, I think five others. On my right, a couple hundred feet, was Stokesey Holmes, in his boat. He was from Texas and very proud of it—always bragging about Texas. We were getting near the beach, and getting daylight, so I saw some bombers. We were supposed to hit the beach with our rockets at 6:06 a.m., D-Day, and we were right on time, but before we got to the beach, I looked up and saw a large group of American bombers coming. And I figured what they were going to do, so I slowed down and I waved for Stokesey Holmes to slow down too. But he either did not see me or ignored me. He went right on. He got to the beach just the same time as those bombers did and that beach was being covered with high powered explosive bombs. That just buried him in sand and dust. The next time I saw him, he was coming out of there just as fast as that boat would get him out. I have no idea whether he put his rockets on the beach or not. But we went on; by the time we went there the dust and sand had cleared, and we put our rockets on the beach as we were supposed to. We fired 48 anti-personnel rockets on the beach. I saw no reaction, no resistance. After that I turned around, and went out to sea, out into the English Channel. And we almost immediately met the first wave of soldiers or GIs to hit the beach.

When I was turned around and coming off the beach, I saw ships anchored in three directions, right, left, and straight ahead. It looked more like a city that anything else. That was one of the greatest thrills in my entire life, to see all those ships anchored there, all of them backing me.

We were the first line of boats to approach the beach that day, and no photographers or reporters were with us, so that is why no one ever saw any pictures of our rocket boats or ever read about us in newspapers or books.

I was at Utah Beach, and it was quiet compared to Omaha, the other beach we invaded. Over at Omaha, the men were just chewed up. I saw very little resistance and our soldiers pushed inland and got off the beach pretty quick.

We were told to tie up to one of the ships sunk on the bottom of the ocean. They had sunk about three ships there to form a little harbor called a Mulberry, protection for small boats. My boat was tied up to it along with several others. How many I have no idea. For about a week my job was to run messages between the ships anchored all out in the Channel. We ate and slept on the ships that made up the Mulberries.

But D-Day plus about six, six days after D-Day, a very severe storm came up. The water got so rough that they were not able to land anything, not any more soldiers, or any supplies were put ashore for a few days. I do not remember how many. Everybody was really upset because we had been supplying the beach. Soldiers were going ashore and marching in a continuous line, single file, non-stop, going inland. But we had none of that for about three days. But as I said, we were tied up to one of the ships, the Mulberry, when that rough weather came about D-Day plus six and broke all the boats loose. Those boats, jumping up and down about ten feet at a time, broke all the lines they were tied with. They drifted into the shore and were beaten to pieces on the shore, including my boat, and everything I had was in that boat except what I was wearing. Of course, I was soon issued other clothing and necessities.

I was told by some of my crew that one of my crew, named Wilton Smith, went ashore and stepped on a land mine and was killed. I never saw him again. We were under strict orders not to go ashore because we did not know where mines or other dangers might be, so we were not supposed to go ashore for any reason. I reported Smith's death to someone in England, but I had difficulty finding someone to take the message (death record attached).

After I was in England a very short time, I boarded a plane for North Africa. I boarded a ship for Italy, where I was slated to skipper another rocket boat for the invasion of Southern France. On the way, someone high up decided he wanted fewer rocket boats and more LCVPs. Me and a few other rocket boat crews were dropped off in Italy. I spent a few weeks in Southern Italy, near Salerno and Rome, and saw how the war had just torn up everything. I think I flew back to North Africa.

There I boarded LST 50 and stayed aboard 50 until almost the end of the war. We came back to New York, and after quite a bit of time being repaired and re-outfitted, we headed through the Panama Canal to Okinawa, and I left Okinawa just a very short time before the war was over. I was on Saipan when the war was over, and what an exciting, wonderful time that was.

Lemuel C. Laney
April 9, 2006

Ensign Lemuel Laney's Crew
Gunner/Motormac Albert W. Coogan and S1c Harry M. Fleisher

Ensign Lemuel C. Laney

I was fortunate to reconnect with two of my crewmates from D-Day in 2007 for the first time in 63 years. After much reminiscing and emotions, they agreed to provide their memories of Utah Beach, 6:00 a.m., D-Day; June 6, 1944. Unfortunately, one of our crew members from D-Day, Wilton Smith, did not survive the Invasion. He was detached from my crew temporarily several weeks after D-Day, and stepped on a land mine at Utah Beach and was killed instantly. He holds the distinction of having served his country on one of the greatest days in its history, but gave his life and never got to appreciate the freedom we fought together for that day. God rest his soul. His report is attached next page.

27 June 1944.

Report on SMITH Wilton (n), 575 89 12, S1c, V-6, USNR, killed by explosion of land mine, due to enemy action, on 21 June 1944, at Utah Beach.

SMITH, was detached from the U.S.S. BAYFIELD (APA-33), 9 June 1944 to S.S. ROBERT-SON, with written orders, and all records and accounts. Orders were not endorsed, or records taken up by U.S. ROBERTSON. SMITH, was doing despatch work for NOIC from U.S.S. LCI 95. SMITH, received verbal orders from Admiral MOON, to return to the U.S.S. BAYFIELD. SMITH and crew could not return due to stormy weather. Boat was sent into Goosberry (near beach) for protection and was lost in storm. SMITH, went ashore, to the seawall or back of it. Later a mine explosion was heard by other crew members. The remains were taken care of by Graves Registration Division, U.S. Army. Identification was made by clothing being worn. The explosion occured about 1400, 21 June 1944.

Remainder of crew, with officer in charge, Ens. L.C. LANEY, returned to U.S.S. BAYFIELD, 22 June 1944. Received verbal orders from the Staff of the U.S.S. BAYFIELD to go to NOIC on U.S.S. LCI 95 for written orders to return to the United Kingdom. Received written orders to report to U. S. NAVAL ADVANCED AMPHIBIOUS BASE, Portland Weymouth, Dorset, arrived 24 June 1944.

Ens. L.C. Laney
Ensign L. C. LANEY, 257 847, D V-G, USNR
Officer-in-Charge, Boat Crew LCS (S) 30.

Gunner Albert W. Coogan

I was born May 14, 1924. I completed my training at Navy Pier, Chicago, as a Motor Machinist, then went on to Solomon's MD and cross-trained as a thirty-caliber machine gunner for LCS(S) Rocket Boats.

Regarding D-Day, as we approached Utah Beach, the tide was high enough that mines we observed low in the water had no effect on our low draft LCS(S) Rocket Boat. We were immediately and continuously under fire upon approach to the beach. I could hear pings of bullets sound off our coxswains fire shield and observed strafing of the water right up to our boat. We were able to get our rockets off, but could not access their damage due to the damage being caused by our battleships. We began our counter attack in which I manned my thirty-caliber and started strafing machine gun nests on the beach and in the cliffs. We pulled back to the Bayfield safely, thank God!

Seaman 1c
Harry M. Fleisher

I, Harry M. Fleisher, born December 5, 1926, came to the Rocket Boat Program by accident. I had been trained thoroughly at Bainbridge, MD for the larger LCT's, but in February 1944 contracted a terrible sinus infection, which hospitalized me for several weeks, and my LCT crew was shipped out. I was then assigned to Ensign Lemuel Laney's crew for Rocket Boat operations in place of Walter Spainhour. When we left for England March 7, 1944, I was the only crew member with no formal training on Rocket Boats. However, I adapted quickly once in England and found myself in one of the most dangerous missions on D-Day; that is, to go into Utah Beach with this small 36-foot boat, one half hour before the troops were to arrive and attack the fortifications on the beaches and cliffs. I can tell you the anticipation of my new duties left me with several sleepless nights. Luckily, by God's grace, we survived the shell and shot of the German 88's.

S2c Larry (Yogi) Berra

Lawrence P. Berra was born in St. Louis, MO, on May 12, 1925, the fourth of five children, to Italian immigrant parents. He would become one of baseball's greatest catchers and most beloved personalities, a genuine American folk hero. Quoted universally for his witty philosophy, "It ain't over till it's over," he has also come to stand for integrity and incomparable dignity.

He was the anchor of the New York Yankee dynasty from the late 1940s to the early 1960s, appearing in 14 World Series and winning more championships (10) than anyone in baseball history. He won Most Valuable Player awards in 1951, 1954, and 1955, and appeared in 15 All-Star Games. According to author Rob Neyer, "Might have been the most respected player of his era."

He was married to Carmen Short on January 26, 1949, and had three sons. They currently have 11 grandchildren.

Yogi is also the inspiration for the Yogi Berra Museum & Learning Center, a nonprofit sports education center on the campus of Montclair State (NJ) University, which teaches students the importance of respect, tolerance, and sportsmanship.

He earned the nickname "Yogi" during his growing up years in St. Louis. His friends had seen a Hindu fakir in a movie, which reminded them of Berra when he sat with his arms and legs folded during his American Legion baseball games.

Yogi was drafted into the Navy in 1943 and was immediately sent to Little Creek, VA, and volunteered for LCS(S) Rocket Boat Training on January 16–31, 1944. He became a Seaman 2c under Ensign Stoke P. Holmes, working off the USS Bayfield on D-Day; the Flagship of Utah Beach, June 6, 1944 (Northern France). He was transferred four weeks later to Ensign Nicholas Zuras for LCS(S) Rocket Boats for the Invasion of Southern France on August 15, 1944 (see Nick Zura's Southern France Summary).

ADVANCE BASE ASSESSMENT AT RAIDERS UNIT
NAVAL TRAINING CENTER
MITO BEACH, LONG ISLAND, NEW YORK

SAILING LIST LCS(S) CREW #26.

OFFICER

1. HOLMES, Stoke P.   Ensign

ENLISTED PERSONNEL.

1. MULTVICE, Michael G.   S2c
2. STRATTON, Jason E.   S2c
3. SULLIVAN, Harold A.   S2c
4. BERRA, Lawrence P.   S2c
5. COULTER, George K.   F1c
6. DUNHAM, John A.   F1c

What follows are my recollections of the Navy at 18 years of age, preparing for D-Day.

Training at Little Creek for small boats amphibious operations was intense, but I became very bored at these small towns. I grabbed the first chance that came along to get out of there. I was sitting in the movies one night, I think watching Clark Gable and Spencer Tracy in a picture called *Boom Town,* when they stopped the movie to make an announcement. They said they were looking for volunteers to serve on a new kind of ship, the LCS(S) Rocket Launcher, and that anybody who was interested should go back to their barracks and tell their commanding officer. I was ready. I got right up and went, and beginning the next day, I didn't have anymore worry about having anything to do.

We trained for five to six weeks. The officers made it clear that we were not going to be spectators in combat. When we saw the boats themselves, we didn't have any doubts. The LCS(S) was 36 feet and carried a six-man crew, and was armed with machine guns and rockets. The boat really wasn't much of anything, except a platform to carry a whole lot of firecrackers. My job was firing the machine gun.

One thing that made us realize that it was serious business we had volunteered for was the fact that we weren't allowed to write a word about what we were doing in our letters home, and the officers kept impressing upon us that we should not say a word about it even to anybody on the base. They didn't think the Germans knew anything about these Top Secret Rocket Launchers yet, and they wanted to keep it that way.

D-Day, June 6, 1944, 4:30 a.m.

It was exactly 4:30 a.m. on the morning of June 6, 1944 when our little boat was lifted up on the davits and lowered over the side of the USS Bayfield. Boat, machine guns, rockets, and six-man crew, everything was expendable as hell, we headed for the rendezvous in front of Omaha Beach, and then our crew, under Ensign Stoke P. Holmes, headed in for Utah Beach at approximately 6:00 a.m. We had maps showing where the German machine gun emplacements were; our job was to let them have it with rockets so that the GIs on LCVPs following us would have a better chance making in onto the beach. The allied airplanes were still pounding the daylights out of the area when we started in. I was only 18 and didn't think anybody could kill me.

We went all the way in to about two to three hundred yards. We had been ordered to watch the lead boat in the group fire a test rocket, and if it reached the beach, then we were all supposed to let go. The first one made it easy; hell, we were closer than the hitter is to the left field screen at Fenway Park. Then we all joined in and it was like nothing I had ever seen before in my life.

My Commanding Officer on D-Day, Ensign Stoke P. Holmes

After unloading our rockets onto Utah Beach at 6:00 a.m. on D-Day, we were diverted between Omaha and Utah Beaches as patrol support, with our machine guns for the additional LCVP landing craft, LCMs, and all other small and large craft protecting the assault troops, as pictured below. We had several confrontations with enemy aircraft over the next several days, unloading our 30 calibers and twin 50's. We wrapped up our final days working off the Bayfield doing various duties in the harbor. The weather and ocean got real rough, nearly sinking our LCS(S). All of our crew survived D-Day and the Normandy Invasion by the grace of God.

Possibly the LCS(S) Rocket Boat PA33-29 from the USS Bayfield I was on, on patrol off Normandy Beach D-Day as verified below by Ensign Lemuel Laney's list of USS Bayfield Rocket Boats. Picture taken by Ensign William H. Palmer, his handwritten LCS boat designation at top of picture

The Rocket Boat pictured above, patrolling off Normandy on or about June 8, 1944, might've been the one I manned during the Normandy Invasion. I can't tell for sure. Ensign William H. Palmer, who I trained with back at Solomons, MD, provided this picture. I really haven't seen an actual picture of an LCS(S) Rocket Boat in action, but this does look similar to my boat.

It's interesting that more information about our secret Rocket Boat Operation came up while this book was in the works. Ensign Lemuel C. Laney (see written summary on page sixty-six) approached Utah Beach parallel to our crew under Ensign Stoke P. Holmes on D-Day at 6 a.m. Ensign Laney's orders for the four USS Bayfield (PA33) officers are dated June 27, 1944. This was three weeks after D-Day. It shows my name listed under Ensign Holmes crew at the top of the orders on LCS(S) Rocket Boat PA33-29 being scratched off the crew. This is when I was transferred for the Invasion of Southern France, August 15, 1944.

Yogi Berra

U. S. NAVAL ADVANCED AMPHIBIOUS BASE
PORTLAND WEYMOUTH, DORSET.

27 June 1944

The following officers and crews, with boats, are scheduled to re
the USS BAYFIELD.

Ensign S. P. HOLMES, D.V(G), USNR PA 33-29.
Rokker, Peter   MoMM 1c
PRILIVICH, M. G.   32c S 1c
SULLIVAN, E. B.   32c S 1c
STRATTON, J. A.   S2c
                       32c MoMM 3c
DUNHAM, J. A.   MoMM3c
DOUTRE, G. L.   MoMM3c

Ensign L. G. LANEY, D.V(G), USNR. PA 33-30
Graham, L.S.   MoMM3c
BAILEY, J. C.   Cox BM 3c
BOUDREAU, B. A.   32c S1c
COOMBS, A. C.   F2c F1c
TABLER, R. E.   F1c
Kaslasky, J.   GM 3c
Lt.(jg) A. F. MIKACZEWSKI, D.V(G), USNR. PA 33-28

KINCASE, Arley D.   MoMM1c
COSELI, Charles   S1c
GLUECKLERT, Elmer   S1c
TOLLOUS, George   F1c
STEWART, Robert   S1c
CLARKSON, Lewis   S1c

ROUDE, J. J.   S2c   PA 33-27
BERGER, Joseph   S2c
MIRASULO, Eugene   S2c
LEVEQUE, Irene   MoMM2c
ROKKER, Peter   MoMM1c
BARKIS, Nolan   Cox

Reported aboard: June 24, 1944. They do not have order as to
ultimate disposition.

Ensign Albert M. Low

Author (Bill Palmer) note:
Periodically, true heroes and leaders come along and our nation is built on their blood. Though he survived the war, Ensign Albert M. Low is an icon and true American hero, having received commendations at Utah Beach, D-Day, and the Silver Star and Purple Heart at Southern France. He and his crew were the quintessential Rocket Boat Crew and spearheaded meeting the goals and objectives of the LCS(S) Rocket Boat Program by their aggressive gallantry and altruism in their missions at Utah and Southern France beaches.

Not only did he live to tell his experiences to his family, but he assiduously recorded them in his memoir. Fortunately, his children, Albert, Patricia, and Pete, have passed them on for the benefit of all brave rocketboatmen, their families, Naval history, and posterity.

Memories of my father, Albert Michael Low
Born in Boston, Massachusetts on August 26, 1921, my father changed the course of his life when he took a hiatus from the University of Indiana to join the Navy. His first responsibility was to become a commissioned officer via the "Ninety Day Wonder" program. In his yet-to-be-published book, he recounts his days as a young officer, having volunteered for extra-long and hazardous duty. His two compelling reasons for doing so: to dispel the commonly held sentiment that Jews were cowards and to assist the Allies in saving the world from Hitler.

His adventures began in New York, where he sought brave men who would relish taking great risks. To this end, he interviewed imprisoned Navy sailors, and freed from the brig those he felt he could trust, men on whose lives his would depend. From America into Europe and Northern Africa he traveled, finding adventure and love. It was also where his 288 tubes of

Woolworth's "Dangerous Red" lipstick, bought on a gambler's whim in New York City, truly earned its name.

After the war, my father returned to university, and graduated from the Wharton School of Business and Finance at the University of Pennsylvania. My parents married in 1946 and moved to Florida, where my father and his brother owned a lawn mower repair shop. However, after the third of their four children was born, they decided to settle in Augusta, GA, his wife's hometown. During the years that my brothers, sister, and I were growing up, my father first worked as salesman in his father-in-law's business. He then built and operated an automatic carwash, and later became a stockbroker for F.I. DuPont and Company.

Having enough success in the stock market to support his retirement, he began traveling the world at the age of 47. Looking again for adventure, he found it; in addition, he found love in the Philippines. He spent his last 25 years in south Florida with his devoted and lovely second wife. Each spring and summer, they'd entice his grown children and our friends onto their sailboat, where they cruised the Bahamas for months at a time.

At home in Pompano Beach, my father's last years were fulfilling ones. He spent his days reading biographies and the classics, listening to beautiful music, playing the stock market, managing his several small strip malls, swimming in the ocean, and writing. His poetry, short stories, and memoirs (many set against the backdrop of World War II) gave each day great purpose and brought him profound satisfaction. He died at the age of 75 on August 16, 1997. Having earned the Silver Star and Purple Heart during his rocket boat missions, he was at peace, knowing he'd be buried in Arlington Cemetery under a tombstone engraved with the Star of David.

The following excerpts are from the memoir of Ensign Albert M. Low, Utah Beach, June 6, 1944. Although the mission descriptions are true, crewmembers' names are fictionalized.

My D-Day story begins with the attack transport USS Dickman which crossed the English Channel in the late evening and early morning of June 5–6, 1944. We were unloaded over the Dickman's side and promptly set up our LCS(S) Rocket Boat.

APA (attack transport) USS Dickman

Photograph supplied by Albert Kiel; Motormac LCS(S) Rocket Boats of USS Bayfield

Our small craft is packed with machine guns, rockets, and its crew of nascent killers. We head toward the hostile shore, intending to clear it for the first wave of infantry: one hundred and eighty soldiers crowded into six LCVPs. They, like conforming pack wolves, follow the leader, perhaps to their deaths. These troops are perhaps the most anxious, but they are certainly the most fearsome and most feared of the Allied Armies.

Utah Beach is the goal. Behind them, crowding the horizon, an awesome armada supports the largest confrontation in the history of mankind. A resolute enemy is dug-in and waiting.

Percussion shakes the world as battleships convulse, firing their most lethal weapons at distant targets. Cordite fumes, turbulent and swirling, issue from the barrel end and hang above the turrets. The trumpet's blast has sounded. Armageddon approaches!

"While looking for the Ancon we came along side and just under the main guns of the HMS Nelson. It started firing broadside just over our heads deafening us".

John H. Schmitt; Motormechanic

A diesel engine pushes LCS(S) 13 past geysers erupting from the sea. Projectiles punch holes through the air, shrieking oncoming slaughter of humans below. Concussions slam our boat from side to side as if it were a mere plaything, rather than ten tons of fighting machine.

Simulated side view of Ensign Albert M. Low's approach on D-Day

"Captain, I'm having a hell of a time keeping 'er on course!"

"Do your best, Sandy."

"Aye aye, Sir."

Ensign Albert M. Low, 22, with two years of college behind him, experiences this encounter with Army First Lieutenant Paul Bitters, who acts as NGLO (Naval Gunfire Liaison Officer), and his Radioman, Corporal Paul Nestor. Six Navy crewmen are at their battlestations: Coxswain Amos Sanderson, Gunners Mate Jack MacAndrews, Motor Mech Lewis Raymond, Signalman Diego Cervone, and Seamen Robert Brown and Clay Ruggles.

NGLO Bitters and Low stand side by side. Corporal Nestor is in the cockpit with his gear.

Each LCVP was intended to carry thirty-six soldiers, or a jeep, with as many men as could squeeze in.

A shell strikes under the boat and explodes. The shock wave knocks Bitters from his feet. He looks up, "We okay, Low? Nobody hurt? The hull, I mean?"

I cut Bitters short with a curt, "Don't worry." There is no time for talk. My responsibility is to land the first wave, but where is Red Beach? Boats are being sunk and men who might be rescued are drowning. Every human instinct cries for me to forego a few minutes' time to save them, but more urgent priorities demand our attention. Within minutes, LCVPs trailing the lead boat will drop their ramps and soldiers will pile out to fight for Europe and their lives. My boat must guide those ramps to the right spot at exactly the right time. Then my crew and I must protect the first wave as they run to gain territory.

H-Hour minus seconds ... bombs saturate the beach. Fireballs streak every which-way. Dirt clouds rise, fires erupt, hostile artillery screams. Concussions shake the world, and men reel.

This is the focal point of the fury of nations. As the contest for a strip of sand advances, steel speeds into mayhem. Boats sink, men fall, fumes rise. Foul odors displace the sweet winds of summer and the scent of death drifts across the land.

Reference landing points A and B should be within the bombed perimeter, but are not. I check and recheck until I am convinced that our airmen have missed the target. They should have dropped their bombs on Red Beach, a mile or so to the northeast.

Gunner's Mate MacAndrews' twin fifty-caliber machine guns are ready to spit hell's fire at anything within range. And, should the opportunity arise, our salvos of well-placed rockets are aimed to send enemy personnel to perdition.

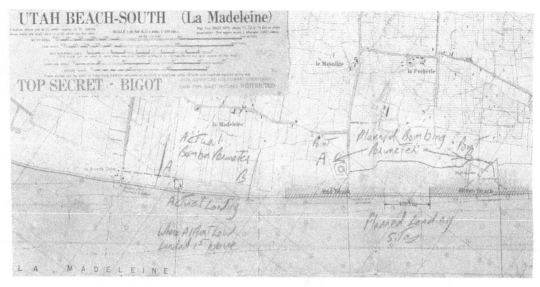

UTAH Beach: Top Secret Bigot Map Planned Bombing and Landing Sites vs. Actual Sites
Map supplied by Ensign Ralph Frede

LCVPs crowd my stern, and behind them press the invasion, millions strong. Do I lead the first wave to the scheduled site or to where waves of bombers have pulverized a strip of sand?

A decision must be made, and I must make it! With but only seconds to consider, let alone analyze, I decide we'll take our chances where the beach was pulverized. As we bear toward the bombed beach, I search for reasons not to. The gradient seems a bit shallow, but looks deep enough. Hedgehogs and floating mines are plainly visible, most of which can be exploded by machine gun fire.

Books I've read indicate that the first wave landed where it did because of sunken control boats and/or powerful riptides. Not true. One of the most junior officers in the United States Navy, exercising his best judgment, landed the first wave where the shoreline had been laid to waste by a devastating air raid.

Author (Bill Palmer) note: Ensign Albert M. Low above clarifies Naval History at Utah Beach on D-Day. Landing three quarters of a mile south of the planned site had nothing to do with powerful currents or strong riptides. Rather on his orders, the landing at Utah Beach took place at the **cleared errant bombed site**. This was an obvious quick intelligent pragmatic solution by Ensign Albert M. Low.

At precisely H-Hour, steel ramps slammed against wet sand. Some men charged from their LCVPs yelling defiance; others, no less brave, pushed quietly toward the enemy; still others dropped for a look-around. Amidst the swoosh of mortars, the whine of enemy artillery, and the staccato of machine guns, the first wave violates fortress Europe. I am worried because the invasion has started from the wrong beach on my say-so! What will the repercussions be?

Enemy soldiers rise from hidden trenches, their weapons pointed seaward. Although many have been wounded or killed, most survive to fight for Fatherland and der Fuehrer. H-Hour is their moment too. With the first wave landed, Sandy at the helm and the crew eager, Rocket Boat 13 skirts the beach to support the invaders. More than once, I'm compelled to implore, "For God's sake, men, don't get too excited. Don't shoot Americans!"

Shadowy shapes in strange uniforms are raked by our machine gun fire. The thirties get so hot they must be handled with rags. Armed with nearly a hundred 4.5-inch rockets, six 30-caliber machine guns, a pair of fifties, and a Thompson automatic, my rocket boat delivers the burn of infuriated bees with a variety of stingers.

Rear and front views of LCS(S) bridge: 30 and 50 caliber guns as they would appear in action. Ensign Cranwell's crew training maneuvers. Picture provided by daughter Elizabeth Cranwell

Bullets strike against the boat's armor and ricochet away; some splitter the plywood hull. Fear of being sunk chills us; yet our mindset remains "Attack!" The ultimate test is at hand. Are we good enough? Will we rise to greatness or settle for less?

I con the boat head-on to shore, all guns ablaze. Defenders fire from their trenches. I yearn to destroy them with rocket salvos, but not wishing to deplete my most powerful weaponry on inconsequential targets, I fire only a few.

Beyond the shoreline, machine gun and mortar emplacements have halted the American advance. We sight the difficulty and dispense dozens of rockets, scoring several hits. Close-to support is needed. I run the boat onto the sand, in effect, making the boat a shoreline pill box. All the while, MacAndrews' twin fifties harass the enemy with machine gun fire.

First wave soldiers, not yet set up, advance slowly or stand by. Meanwhile, troops from the second and third waves reach shore and work their way toward the berm. The waves integrate and the enemy is overcome.

A couple of hundred yards to the southwest, Rocket Boat 13 comes across what appears to be the Army's most advanced penetration. We expect troops to signal recognition, but they ignore us.

I turn to NGLO Bitters, "F'God's sake, radio them."

"I can't," he replies, pointing to his walkie-talkie. A bullet has ripped into it. Had it not been by his ear, his head would have been smashed.

So close! The hair at the back of my neck stiffens. After much waving of hands and pointing to NGLO, his corporal and the radio, someone ashore remembers about the rendezvous. A sergeant waves us in.

As Sanderson touches the boat's bow to the beach, Bitters and his radioman run ashore, consult, receive new equipment, and come back. Thus is communication established between Army First Lieutenant Willis, ashore with his platoon, Navy Ensign Low, commanding a support boat, and his Naval Gunnery Liaison Officer, First Lieutenant Bitters. With Senior Officer Lieutenant Willis in charge, the team is code-named "Able/One." Officers and men all face an enemy for the first time.

Following First Lieutenant Willis' instructions, I station my boat about a hundred yards ahead of the infantry. According to my Navy Intelligence Supplement, our first encounter will be with "Position Dud," a dummy mock-up.

As we approach "Position Dud," what was intended to look like a gun barrel, and it may have from a greater distance, appears to be the trunk of a recently felled tree. Canvas, stretched across framework, is painted to look like a utility shack. Down to plywood cutouts for wheels, the entire scheme seems amateurish. We laugh at the crudeness of it.

Amused and careless, I con for a closer view. The crack-crack-crack of a machine gun spurting bullets nearly panics us. Splashes mark the limit of the gun's range, and thank God for it!

The enemy has fired too soon, a mistake that will cost him dearly.

Bitters takes bearings and calls for destroyer fire. A shell explodes behind the emplacement. Soldiers materialize from hidden positions. Canvas is shucked. An enemy team jumps into action. The "log" splits, exposing a gun barrel. Plywood cutouts are discarded and the gun is loaded, trained, elevated, fired. Rocket Boat 13 is the target.

Sonics crack the air; one projectile, then another, yet another and another, rush toward us, all death intended. Slam! A gash opens along the foredeck down to the water line. Part of the bow is blown away. Had the shot struck lower, the boat would have sunk. A half-dozen yards aft, officers and crew would have been killed. That our boat still floats and that we are alive is a kiss from Lady Luck.

A barrage emits from the fleet, and the enemy's emplacement, with all its artillery and machine guns, is destroyed. Bewildered survivors crawl from their dugout, hands above their heads, anxious to surrender. Bodies not yet stiff are laid on the ground, oozing life's blood, food for ants and creepers.

Strong Point A is a fortified house. Walls have been reinforced with three or more feet of concrete. Trenches radiate outward, as if from the hub of a giant wheel, except where the fortification borders the ocean. German infantry man the strong point; but because their heavy pieces have been disabled by bombardment, they are vulnerable. When Lieutenant Willis discovers that they lack operable weapons with the range of our twin-fifties, he relays that Able/One's rocket boat could attack with impunity.

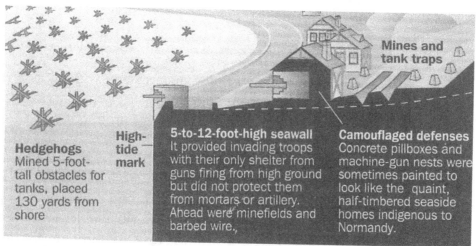

Strong Point A: Fortified house similar on both Utah and Omaha beaches

We clobber the target. As debris settles, the land section for Able/One advances close enough to launch grenades through the strong point's windows. In short order, the defenders are stunned or dead.

As we advance toward Strong Point B, we engage in many of the same procedures with similar results. If a target is big enough, NGLO calls for destroyer gunfire, which, as the operation continues, becomes reasonably accurate.

In due time we reach Strong Point B, another fortified house. Lieutenant Willis calls for destroyer fire but the response is excessively long and worse, the accuracy is unreliable. That many Americans soldiers weren't killed by our own guns was by the grace of God, not the destroyer's gunnery officer. With highly charged optimism after our showing at Strong Point A, Rocket Boat 13 takes on its second strong point, which is soon bested with our rocket and machine gun fire.

There had, however, been terrible losses at Point A. Thirty-three ton Sherman M4-A4 DD tanks had been modified for the D-Day landings at Normandy. They'd been made amphibious, able to churn through seawater to the shore with the use of canvas skirts over wood shoring to keep them afloat. One had been lost to enemy gunfire; another had been assuming position to help us when it was struck by Navy gunfire. Either ship's gunners aimed at a tank they identified as "enemy," or they'd hit our tank by mistake. In both cases, the losses were total and grievous.

DD tank destroyed by enemy fire; over 30 sunk going into Omaha and Utah due to faulty, insufficient floatation devices

Strong Point C was set so tightly against a hill and was so integrated into its surroundings that it was impossible to determine where the building began or ended. A camouflaged casement, undetectable from seaward, afforded sweeping coverage up and down both sides of the beach. Pre-invasion bombardment had disabled its big guns. And although the cannons had been blown askew, lesser weaponry remained operative.

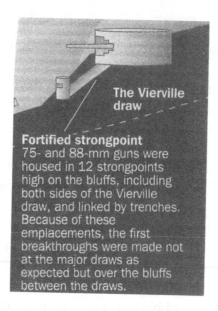

The Vierville draw

Fortified strongpoint
75- and 88-mm guns were housed in 12 strongpoints high on the bluffs, including both sides of the Vierville draw, and linked by trenches. Because of these emplacements, the first breakthroughs were made not at the major draws as expected but over the bluffs between the draws.

Strong Point C: sweeping coverage of the beach, the big guns were 75 and 88 mm

While I was positioning for a frontal attack, about sixteen hundred yards from shore, we began getting clobbered. The Strong Point's still serviceable weaponry had half again the range of ours. Recognizing a losing situation, I order a fast retreat. It would be suicide to challenge them head-on.

STRAFING

Lieutenant Willis orders us to motor beyond the Strong Point to report the lay of the land. That done, and the information relayed, Army Lieutenants Willis and Bitters confer. With much referencing to maps, they decide that Able/One will infiltrate the Strong Point from both sides and from the rear. Some weakness will show up, they conclude, and the platoon would take advantage of it. My boat is to attack from the front.

I argue that the plan is suicidal! If by chance my boat reaches as far as the thousand yard mark, the entire crew, including NGLO and his radioman, will be dead or wounded. Again the Army officers confer. This time they're of different opinions. Bitters, baleful at having been rebuffed, shifts the radio to me. As I begin to express my objections, Willis interrupts, "Pal, you've got your orders. Attack from the front."

Were I Catholic, I'd have crossed myself.

The lead detail began beating its way beyond the berm to infiltrate from the rear. Another is doing the same from the far side; Rocket Boat 13, the diversion, is to proceed dead on from the couple thousands yards out, and to fire rockets and machine guns when within range.

I consult with MacAndrews, "How about it, Gunner, any ideas?"

Without cracking a smile, although the humor was apt, he replies, "Sir, let's get the hell away from this place."

We laugh sardonic laughs. If we get close enough, we could engage; otherwise, our best tactic would be to hug the deck and pray.

At "the word," with tongue dry and damning Lieutenant Willis' strategy, I con LCS(S) 13 to full-speed and head toward shore, straight on.

The sight of an enemy boat rushing toward their guns must have set the Germans to salivating. At seventeen hundred yards, tracers wing toward us. At sixteen hundred, shots ping off our front armor; at fifteen hundred yards, more hits; and at fourteen hundred, bullets slam against the armor plate with the impact of sledgehammers.

The "diversion" had to continue for another three hundred yards. At that distance, presuming the boat was still afloat, we could fire rockets. The military operation was the diversion; the personal operation was survival.

"Damn it, Sandy, run it faster!"

"Tell Raymond," he shouted.

And then I learn something that had never been done, could be done. In a matter of seconds, Raymond disabled the governor, increasing our RPMs. The engine roared to its highest pitch and the boat surged to its fastest speed, all the while getting closer to heavy caliber metal pounding against the hull.

"We're getting close, MacAndrews!"

With an "okay boss" look, he climbs into the machine gun mount without saying a word. I was glad he didn't, because if there were a right time for a sensible man to disobey orders, this would be it. While the rest of us might duck behind armor plate, MacAndrews would be exposed, and would remain exposed until he was hit, or the boat sank, or we were beyond enemy range.

Simulated MacAndrews on twin 50 caliber guns
Picture provided by Robert A. Cannon of his Gunner Ed Zarzynski, Omaha Beach

The closer we get, the more the Germans dump on us. Bullets ricochet from our armor like hailstones bouncing from a tin roof.

I fire my ranger, which lands short, as it is intended to do. MacAndrews' twin fifties are

yap-yapping continuously. I count what seems an endless ten seconds, then fire a full salvo. A humongous explosion follows. Megatons of earth rise, then collapse. Strong Point C settles to rubble. Maybe a rocket had run through an opening to an ammunition magazine. *Maybe anything,* but the improbable has happened: Strong Point C is gone and we are still alive. A German soldier lies dead outside a machine gun emplacement he so vainly defended on

Utah Beach near Les Dunes de Madeleine.

Almost stupefied, we watch with wonderment as the rubble and smoke settle. I suspect none of us believe we've lived through the diversion.

MacAndrews' body lies slumped over his gun, a crease across his skull oozing blood. I pass the first-aid kit to Cervone, who dusts the bloody area with sulphur powder and winds a bandage around the gunner's head. Later, none the worse for the experience, MacAndrews exclaimed, "Hey! I got the Purple Heart."

Telling our diversion story has been short and easy, but living it was anything but, especially for Lieutenant Bitters. If he was going to die in this war, he'd want it to happen on land with his troops, certainly not at sea.

Raymond reports that leakage through the hull is slight enough to be handled by our bilge pumps. He suspects that we have enough fuel to last three or four hours; if lucky, even five. Sanderson reports that the bow damage "is nasty, but not disabling." Ruggles, smiling like the hick he is, added, "This here boat's took more fuck'n hits than the big kettle from a rev'n'ooer's raid."

Our boat has absorbed, or fended off, hundreds of strikes, and a major hit, yet remains seaworthy. Officer and men have become battle-tempered, and we are better for it.

We soon assist as a decoy for Strong Points D and E, similar fortifications. Again, we were told to drive straight on, from a mile or so out, drawing machine gun fire, thus exposing the enemy's encampment to the NGLO on a battleship. The Infantry then could sneak in with grenades to obliterate these positions.

Our final D-Day assignment is Strong Point F, nine miles west. It is double circled, the highest priority target. Photographs, surely sighted through a periscope, picture a casement so massive, it seems fit for burying Egyptian pharaohs. We work steadily with NGLO. After much calibration and coordination, the button is pushed, electrons surge through circuits, fuel ignites, and rockets soar. Twenty-four birds from hell roar skyward, bunched like crowded lemmings aloft. They rush toward a flesh-ravaging end, and we cheer. "Bravo, molto bene," Cervone's voice rises above the clamor.

Moments later, we receive a "well done" from Lieutenant Willis, ashore.

Strong Point F, our sixth major target on D-Day, is eliminated and we are finished.

The Quintessential Rocketboatmen:
Ensign Albert M. Low and Crew

Top, from left: S2c Thomas J. Dolan, Ensign Albert M. Low, S2c Clinton E. Birch
Bottom left/right: MoMM3c Charles R. Rew/William L. Ford/S2c Jerry J. Bergamo
Most photos provided by Clinton E. Birch. Pictures of William Ford and Thomas Dolan provided by sons.

UNITED STATES FLEET
UNITED STATES NAVAL FORCES IN EUROPE
20 Grosvenor Square
London, W.1.

From: Commander TWELFTH Fleet.
To :   Ensign Albert M. Low, D-V(G),
         United States Naval Reserve.

Subj: Commendation.

1.   Your performance of duty as Officer in Charge of a
Landing Craft, Support (Small), while attached to the U.S.S.
▬▬▬▬▬▬▬▬▬, during the amphibious operations on the
coast of Cotentin Peninsula, June 6, 1944, has been brought
to my attention. You ably directed the maneuvering of your
boat, while under enemy fire, to support the landing with
rocket and machine gun fire and then continued this support
from the flank of the beach until assault troops had
consolidated their beach positions.

2.   For your professional ability and leadership in this
connection you are hereby commended.

3.   This commendation carries with it the privilege of
wearing the commendation ribbon.

4.   A copy of this letter will be forwarded to the Chief
of Naval Personnel to be filed in your official record.

Harold R Stark

HAROLD R. STARK,
Admiral, U.S. Navy.

LCS(S) Crew # 26
Ensign Robert Goldsmith

James J. Houde, Seaman 2c, was born August 8, 1924, in New Haven, CT, where he still resides. He was married to Rosy Monaco on September 20, 1947. They had three children. He worked 27 years for Armstrong Weber Company, a truck tire manufacturer, manufacturing tires. He enlisted in late 1943 and proceeded to Little Creek, VA. He was immediately assigned to small boats, amphibious forces; LCS(S) Rocket Boat Program. He became part of LCS(S) Rocket Boat Crew No. 28, under Ltjg. Robert H. Goldsmith, who had one year previously led one of the first waves with his Rocket Boat into Sicily, July 1943. He and his crew disembarked from the USS Bayfield on D-Day. Ensign Goldsmith had been promoted to a Ltjg. James Story at Utah Beach, though Short provides some unique and interesting experiences.

Ltjg. Robert H. Goldsmith

James J. Houde S2c

My Story by James J. Houde S2c

I really never got to know Ltjg. Robert H. Goldsmith that well until we later in England where we were made up for the boat crew with another fellow from West Haven, where I came from. His name was Gene Girasuolo. He's passed away now. While we were in England, that's where Rocket Boat Crew was made up, five crew members and one officer, who was a lieutenant who had experience in the Sicily Invasion, we picked up our Rocket Boat in Dartmouth England. While we were there we stayed at Dartmouth College. We also had an air raid while we were there. They blew a bugle for an alarm. From there we went to Weymouth, England. We stayed at an apartment. We had some repairs done on the boat by an English carpenter. Then we went to an ammunition depo; they mounted two 30-caliber machine guns and a gun turret with two twin 50-caliber machine guns. They loaded rocket mounts on the side of the boat.

When we were at Plymouth, England, we had two air raids by Germany. One was at the bus depo, which the bomb hit. Another one was when we're on the boat. Now we were transported to the invasion of Normandy by USS Bayfield, which was a coast guard ship, which is something like a main office. Our boat was hanging over the side of the ship. We got to the invasion, we were dropped into the water, without the ship ever stopping. We had to be alert, because if we [didn't], the boat would be dragged. Then we wouldn't be able to get unhooked. It was a very dark morning, pitch black, couldn't see your hands in front of you. After the boats got unhooked, they made a circle. This is how we got set by going to the beach.

Going to the beach, it was so messy there, lots of bodies in the water, some were dead and some were alive. We picked up the living, we didn't have time for the dead. This happened after we shot the rockets. An officer on one of the ships yelled, "Pick up the bodies," which we did. We only had a small boat, so all we could pick up were the living. You can take orders, but if it's not possible, we couldn't do it. This is when I heard one of the rocket boats broke down. A crew member stepped on a land mine, from Ensign Lemuel Laney's crew. Another one got machine gunned. When all this was happening, the weather was real bad. The larger ships were off the coast, firing the large guns, as we were going on to the beach. While the big shells were buzzing over our heads, it was kind of a scary noise. Now on the beach, there was a large circle of barbed wire; five women were in the middle of it. They were French women. I asked the soldier on guard why they were in there. He told me they were snipers for the Germans. What made the invasion really messy was how bad the weather was. I guess the weather was what made it good for an invasion, being dark. A lot of German prisoners were taken. We looked down the beach and saw a big black line. The German prisoners were being taken. One soldier told me he heard a noise, turned around, and saw a German soldier standing behind him with his hands up, wanting to be taken in.

Sicily 1946

James Houde

Ensign Stuart P. Hurley

"Silent Hero"

Ensign Stuart P. Hurley, Silent Hero, Utah Beach, June 6, 1944. Provided by daughter Joan Hurley Covelli

My dad, Ensign Stuart P. Hurley, on left

My father first spoke of his D-Day experiences the last time my sister, brother, and I saw him, days before his death. He passed away in 2002 at the age of 80. He married my mom, Charlotte Chick Hurley, in 1947, and had four children. His career after the war was in sales and he was pretty successful. But he suffered from depression and it was believed, in part, due to his experiences in World War II. In the last days of his life, he told us a little about Utah Beach, D-Day, 1944. Though proud of his service, he said it was the most terrible time of his life. Later he was involved in the Invasion of Southern France and in Philippine Liberation Day. He was preparing to invade Japan when the bomb was dropped, confiding in my mother later that he felt his luck with the invasions had run out and the war's end a huge relief. Dad told us of ferrying of soldiers on D-Day, but not of commanding his Rocket Boat earlier that morning. It was not until I was contacted by the author of this book that I discovered his amazing story. I wrote to the Navy, obtained the documents of his service, specifically the "Commendation" he was given for commanding his Rocket Boat and crew in the waters off Utah Beach, while under fire, to provide machine gun support for the landing of the first wave of soldiers on D-Day. Dad was certainly courageous, a hero in a real sense to his family, as he never spoke of, or expected, special treatment for his service. He did simply what was necessary, "A Silent Hero." Dad brought his crew back alive, one of 24 boats that first approached Normandy Beach at 6 a.m., D-Day, June 6, 1944.

TRAN 13 FEBRUARY 1944
LIDO BEACH NY FPT

6 LCSS CREWS

ATTWOOD CURTIS L   ENS

SCHINDLER FRANCIS   FS2C   7587086
BRIDGERS LEON B   S2C   8339069
PAYNE BETHEL M   S2C   8459965
MAQUIN JOHN H   F1C   8525867
ALLUMS ALBERT J JR S1C   6048677
ASCHTGEN DONALD L   F2C   7207268
                                    6

SMITH GEORGE F   ENS

COOKE JAMES T   S2C   8353927
BARKER DELBERT F   S2C   8953005
STEFFY JOSEPH J   S2C   6186991
DIXON JOHN C   F1C   6226701
KEENAN FRANKLIN J   S1C   6175590
EWING FLOYD E JR   F2C   8765538

LOW ALBERT M   ENS

MC CANDLESS C G JR F1 MOM8221456
BERGAMO JERRY J   S2C   6155316
REW CHARLES R JR   MOM3C6055887
DOLAN THOMAS J   S2C   8119026
BIRCH CLINTON E   S2C   6674089
FORD WILLIAM L   S1C   6092425
                                    6

DAILY JAMES L   ENS

ANGEL LEE O   S1C   8333489
RASMUSSEN HERBERT   F1 MOM6525178
LELLINDIA JOHN A   F2 MOM7109485
ELLISON ROY   S2C   6135217
BARROWS HENRY R   S2C   8008869
ARCHIBALD M B JR   S2C   8306735
                                    6

DESMOND FRANCIS J   ENS

PAICH RUDOLPH   COX   8225635
DEPPE ROBERT W   S2C   2497379
NORRIS CHARLES J   S2C   8952166
RISCHENOLE SAMUEL   JS2C   8060375
O MALLEY WILLIAM H F2 MOM8578983
CHYZEL KENNETH W   MOM3C8053944

HURLEY STUART P   ENS

HAMNETT ARTHUR C   S2C   8952996
GUERINT JOSEPH F   S2C   8581140
HAWKINS PAUL E   S2C   8952991
LACH ROBERT F   F2C   7111481
BEAVERS JESSE C   S2C   6356323
FUKA EMIL J   F2C   8768238

NOTICE OF SEPARATION FROM U. S. NAVAL SERVICE
NAVPERS-553 (REV. 8-45)

OFFICER SEPARATION CENTER
BOSTON 14, MASS.

267785   HURLEY, STUART PALMER

LT.(JG) D   18 SAMSON RD.
USNR   MEDFORD (MIDDLESEX)
                MASS.

CHARACTER OF SEPARATION   HONORABLE:
RELEASED FROM ACTIVE DUTY
SAME AS #4

RACE W   SEX M   MARITAL STATUS SINGLE   U.S. CITIZEN YES
DATE AND PLACE OF BIRTH MEDFORD (MIDDLESEX) MASS. 10 AUG.1921

HOME ADDRESS AT TIME OF ENTRY INTO SERVICE 29 COTTAGE ST., MEDFORD, MASS.

MEANS OF ENTRY ENLISTED

DATE OF ENTRY INTO ACTIVE SERVICE 6 JULY 1943

7TH MAR '42   28 OCT '43

PLACE OF ENTRY INTO ACTIVE SERVICE USNMS, ABBOTT HALL, CHICAGO, ILL.

NET SERVICE (3) 5/6/45

QUALIFICATIONS COMMANDING OFFICER

RATINGS HELD

FOREIGN AND/OR SEA SERVICE WORLD WAR II X YES

SERVICE SCHOOLS COMPLETE USNMS, ABBOTT HALL, CHICAGO, ILL.   16

VESSELS AND STATIONS SERVED ON
USS JOSEPH T. DICKMAN (APA 13)
USS LST 406
USS LST 288
USS LST 610

PAY   EST AUGUST $58.20 KLP   SEPT. $100.00 6.60 YES   C.B. COTTON BO232

AMERICAN THEATRE
ASIATIC PACIFIC (1 STAR)
EUROPEAN AFRICAN (2 STARS)
VICTORY WORLD WAR II
LTR. OF COMMENDATION
PHILIPPINE LIBERATION
SOCIAL SECURITY #

Robert H. Preston
ROBERT H. PRESTON, LT.COMDR., USNR

MAIN CIVILIAN OCCUPATION STUDENT IN COLLEGE

JOB PREFERENCE
BUSINESS
NO LOCALITY PREFERENCE

COMM. B R.R. 4 CO. 4 AB LANGUAGES

20 SEPT. 1946   Stuart P. Hurley
DATE OF SEPARATION   STUART P. HURLEY, LT. (JG) USNR
                       SIGNATURE OF PERSON BEING SEPARATED

UNITED STATES FLEET
UNITED STATES NAVAL FORCES IN EUROPE
20 Grosvenor Square
London, W.1.

From: Commander TWELFTH Fleet.
To   :   Ensign Stuart P. Hurley, D-V(G),
         United States Naval Reserve.

Subj: Commendation.

1.   Your performance of duty as Officer in Charge of a
Landing Craft Support (Small), while attached to the U.S.S.
JOSEPH T. DICKMAN, during the amphibious operations on the
coast of Cotentin Peninsula, June 6, 1944, has been brought
to my attention. You ably directed the maneuvering of
your boat under enemy fire to support the landing with
rocket and machine gun fire and then continued this support
from the flank of the beach until the assault troops had
consolidated their beach positions.

2.   For your professional ability and leadership in this
connection you are hereby commended.

3.   This commendation carries with it the privilege of
wearing the commendation ribbon.

4.   A copy of this letter will be forwarded to the Chief
of Naval Personnel to be filed in your official record.

                        HAROLD R. STARK,
                        Admiral, U.S.Navy.

FINISHED FILE PERS 332

95

CHAPTER 8

D-Day Operation Overload at Omaha Beach
Northern France
June 6, 1944

Ensigns Curtis L. Attwood, Edwin H. Lemkin,
Herman F. Vorel, Nicholas J. Zuras, Gunner Bethel Payne,
Coxswain George A. Bosler

Ensign Curtis L. Attwood

LCS(S) Rocket Boat Summaries and Maps
of
Ensign Curtis L. Attwood, Gunner; Bethel M. Payne
Ensign Herman F. Vorel and Coxswain George Bosler
Ensigns Nicholas J. Zuras, Edwin H. Lemkin, Robert A. Cannon

Six Ensigns and from Omaha Beach LCS(S) Rocket Boat Missions

Ensigns Robert A. Cannon,
Herman F. Vorel, Edwin H. Lemkin,
Nicholas J. Zuras

Ensign Elmer "Chick" Oist
USS Samuel Chase

Omaha Beach
6:00 a.m. June 6th 1944

Ensign Curtis L. Attwood

Ensign Curtis L. Attwood was born August 13, 1921, in New Edinburgh, AR. He graduated Arkansas A&M (now University of Arkansas, Monticello) in 1943, with a bachelor's in Business Administration. He became a district sales representative for Entergy Corporation (39 years). He married Billie Jo Welch on January 15, 1948. They had two children, a son and a daughter. He retired in 1986. He passed away on January 10, 2001.

His story is unique at Omaha and created a great backdrop into the Omaha Beach Invasion. Besides being on an LCS(S) Rocket Boat that went into Fox Green Beach at 6:00 a.m., D-Day, he was sent into Fox Green Beach several hours earlier that morning with the Scouts and Raiders on a reconnaissance mission. He was sent in to identify German gun emplacements on the beach and obstacles in the water; obstructions that must be cleared by the demolition units for the easy access to Fox Green Beach for the LCS(S) Rocket Boat Missions to take place at dawn.

The map below provides a good view to all of Omaha Beach, marking out Ensign Attwood's point of entry to Fox Green by the French town of Coleville-Sur-Mer, France, between 2:00 and 4:00 a.m., D-Day.

It cannot be overstated that Ensign Curtis L. Attwood's mission into Omaha was tenuous. He reiterated this story to his son several times over the years and it became vivid in his memory and provided one of our most ominous and authentic documents of this book: the view of Fox Green Beach at Omaha and the infamous Church Steeple at Coleville-Sur-Mer; reference point for the Invasion Boats. It is best that we now listen to his son's story of his father's mission on D-Day.

Stories my father, Ensign Curtis L. Attwood, told me of his D-Day Missions at Omaha Beach.

One story my father related to me, I always thought had occurred a couple of nights prior to the Invasion, but Dad's pastor related that Dad had told him a few years before that it was the morning of June 6, 1944. Before daylight, Dad and several other crew members had gone ashore to "tag" obstacles (his term, i.e., place charges to blow up). While on the beach, they began taking sporadic small arms fire from the German positions above the beach. As it was still dark, the fire was ineffective, but close enough to delay them. Dad believed that the Germans did not even know what they were shooting at.

At this, Dad was separated from the two men he was with. By his description, a large black man appeared down the beach, moving in his direction. As the man reached him, flopped down at his side, Dad heard him say, "Don't worry, Ensign, your gonna be okay!" With that, Dad said the man got up and proceeded down the beach and into the darkness. Dad said he did not know the man and had never seen him before. He was not one of the crew members Dad was familiar with, and Dad never saw him again. Efforts to find him after the chaos of the invasion were fruitless. Dad became convinced that the man was an angel sent to reassure him that all would be well. Only in the last few years have I appreciated the fact that my father was one of a very few men that was actually on Omaha Beach on the morning of D-Day, before the invasion ever began.

by son Fred Attwood

Invasion Map of Ensign Curtis L. Attwood utilized early a.m. June 6, 1944 at Fox Green Beach, Omaha

Invasion Map of Ensign Curtis L. Attwood utilized early a.m. June 6" 1944 at Fox Green Beach; Omaha

CHURCH
686882

COLVILLE-SUR-MER
(687882)

Omaha Beach Fox Green Beach near Coleville Church steeple reference point for troop landings and gun emplacements as witnessed by Ensign Curtis L. Attwood June 5-6th 1944

A second story my father told me pertained to his LCS(S) Rocket Boat Mission at 6:am D-Day at Fox Green Beach. He said he was sitting off the beach during the first wave, providing support machine gun fire, and was in such awe of the enormity and loudness of the Invasion. He had to remind himself to keep firing. He felt like a small drop in a flood. He could not even hear his own machine gun, the only time he personally fired a machine gun in battle.

by son Fred Attwood

S. P.
687894
(3 LT GUNS)

Bethel M. Payne, Gunner

I, Bethel M. Payne, was born October 26, 1924, in Black Water, VA. I worked at Borden Textiles for 45 years; 30 years as a foreman. I was married to Maryellen Kinsler in 1945. We have one son. I retired in 1996 and live in Kingsport, TN.

I was a gunner and back-up coxswain under Ensign Curtis L. Attwood. I was under his command for LCS(S) Rocket Boat training in Solomon's, MD, through D-Day. On June 6, 1944, our crew crossed the Channel on an LST with three other Rocket Boat crews. Below is a list of our crew and to the right my picture. Francis Schindler was our coxswain.

Bethel M. Payne; Gunner

```
ATTWOOD CURTIS L        ENS

SCHINDLER FRANCIS  FS2C
BRIDGERS LEON D        SFC
PAYNE BETHEL M         S2C
BROLIN JOHN H          F1C
ALLUMS ALBERT J JR SIC
ASCHTGEN LOWALD L      F2C
```

Ensign Curtis L. Attwood LCS(S) Crew

I was not part of my Ensign's group, Scouts and Raiders, that went into Fox Green Beach at Coleville-Der-Sur at 3:00 a.m. on D-Day to tag obstacles. However, I saw major action as a gunner there at Fox Green Beach at 6:00 a.m. on D-Day, under Ensign Curtis L. Attwood.

At 6:00 a.m. on D-Day, June 6, 1944, we debarked from our LST and proceeded into Fox Green Beach at Omaha. I helped load and fire all 48 rockets. I observed a scattered pattern; some rockets even landing in the woods.

Immediately after the rockets were fired, we closed in on the beach and beached our boat. The noise of the machine guns and bombings was so great, I could not hear myself talk. The smoke from all the bombing from the destroyers left little visibility. But out of the corner of my right eye, I noticed what appeared to be sparklers. I took a closer look and noticed a German Pillbox firing in our direction. I then started noticing these same sparklers out of my left eye and observed a second German Pillbox. We were in the middle of a crossfire. We decided that these pillboxes must be eliminated, or the LCVP carrying our first troops would be decimated. Ping, ping, ping was the sound of machine gun bullets bouncing off our boat.

I next climbed up into the harness of the twin 50-caliber machine gun and rotated to my right and pointed at those sparklers in the pillbox on the right. I commenced heavy firing, observing smoke puffs of the bullets bouncing off the concrete pillbox. Our 50-caliber rounds had three different type of bullets. The first bullet was steel; meant to kill individual enemy personnel. The second was an incendiary bullet that exploded on impact. The third was a tracer bullet that would allow you to correct the direction of your firing.

The tracer bullets allowed me to narrow my shooting pattern into the actual hole where the sparklers were coming from. I let into that hole about 100 rounds; before you know it, the sparklers stopped and the pillbox was neutralized. I believe this was due to the incendiary shells that got into the pillbox, exploding and killing the German enemy machine gunners. I [next] concentrated on pillbox 2, on my left. This pillbox was neutralized also. This helped the LCVPs with troops who were now landing.

Bethel M. Payne
12-6-06

Bethel M. Payne, Gunner
under Ensign Curtis L. Attwood

This was our other gunner, Donald Lee Aschtgen, on D-Day at Omaha Beach.

F2c Gunner Donald L. Aschtgen
Born July 28, 1925
Deceased April 8, 1994
Broomfield, CO

Ensign Herman F. Vorel

Herman F. Vorel was born in Peabody, MA, on October 17, 1921. He was one of five children, born of German decent. He attended Boston College and graduated in 1943 with a B.S. in Chemistry. After the war, in 1949, he obtained a master's degree in Chemistry via the G.I. Bill. He immediately started working for Merck & Company Pharmaceuticals as a chemist in their Quality Control Division for over 35 years, and retired in 1985. He retired to Cape Cod and as of the printing of this book is still active, working out three days a week at Willy's Gym in South Orleans, MA.

He was always proud being of German decent, and of taking an active role in the defeat of Hitler and Nazi Germany.

S1c Cleveland Walker, Ensign Herman F. Vorel, S2c Donald Hartman

Ensign Herman F. Vorel with microphone in window at Lido Beach, Long Island, February 1944
Front row: Ensign Stoke P. Holmes, Robert Goldsmith
Back row: Ensign Max Soulier, William Martin, Frank Crawford

My memories of D-Day are faint. I was able to obtain a camera through the Invasion of Normandy and was able to provide the great pictures that follow. I was fortunate that I was reunited this year with George Bosler, my coxswain throughout D-Day and the Normandy Invasion. This was the first I had talked to him in over 60 years. His memory is better than mine and he was able to best summarize our actions on D-Day at Omaha Beach at 6:00 a.m. in his summary on the pages that follow.

Ensign Herman F. Vorel

Coxswain George A. Bosler

George A. Bosler was born in Philadelphia, PA, on April 29, 1925. He was one of three children born of German-English decent. He worked for Philadelphia Electric for over 41 years, ordering and keeping track of inventory as a store clerk. He married Doloros Houston on September 5, 1953. They had two children, boys. He currently resides in Swathmore, PA.

S2c Donald Hartman, Coxswain George A. Bosler,
S1c Joseph Wright

My LCS(S) Crew at Teignmouth, England
Top: Donald Hartman S2c, Milton Scnall, Motormac
Middle: Joseph Wright S1c, George Bosler, Coxswain
Front: Cleveland Walker S1c
Pictures taken by Ensign Herman F. Vorel

Our Story
George A. Bosler, Coxswain
Under Ensign Herman F. Vorel

It was with great surprise to hear that you were living in Old Cape Cod. It was really great talking to you about some of our experiences on our LCS(S) Rocket Boat. I think out boat number was No. 4, but don't hold me to it. The six crewmember names on the small photo are as follows:

Top:
Coxswain George Bosler
Ensign Herman Vorel
MoMM2c Milton Schnall
Bottom:
S1c Joseph Wright
S1c Cleveland Walker
S2c Donald Hartman

As you said before, one great crew.

George and Milton were on shore patrol duty on trains going to New York City from Lido Beach until we left for overseas.

When we arrived in England, we were sent to Teignmouth, Devon, for more LCS(S) training. After training, we were sent to the next port, which was Portsmouth, to be assembled to receive instructions and maps of installations of gun placements. In the meantime, enemy planes flew over, dropping mines. On Sunday, one LCP full of men going to church, blew up, killing quite a few men.

When we were preparing to leave England on the 5th of June, they held us up to the next day, June 6, because of rough seas. We were dropped off about 2:00 a.m., around 6 or 8 miles off the coast of Normandy. When we were close to shore, we picked our targets according to our maps and fired our smoke rockets for distances; then we proceeded to bombard the targets and the beach. After firing our rockets on the beach and gun targets, we returned to escort the waves of the landing crafts filled with soldiers and small vehicles by laying smoke screens in a cross pattern in front of them. We were fired upon by machine guns and 88-mm cannons, so we had to zigzag back and forth to try and avoid their fire. Although we were hit a few times by machine gun fire, nobody was injured and there was no significant damage to our boat. Then we patrolled the sea to see if anybody needed anymore fire power or help. We also picked up survivors or those who were dead from the waters. We took them to any LST flying a Mike flag for medical aid or other help, as needed. Our boat could be picked up by any LST that had a boat davit room. Once picked up, we would help them in any way we were instructed.

Afterwards, we waited for our next assignment, which was Southern France, Marseilles, and Toulon. We performed the same duties as Normandy.

Two crewmen holding bullet ridden Old Glory after coming back from Omaha Beach at 6:00 a.m. D-Day. Picture taken by Ensign Herman Vorel

This was a picture taken of an LST being sunk on D-Day, Omaha Beach Picture provided by Ensign Robert A. Cannon

This is me, Ensign Herman F. Vorel, next to a destroyed tank on a downtown road in France

Ltjg. Vorel, later on as oversight officer in 1945, as Japanese prisoners getting frisked in Tsingtao, China

Ensign Edwin H. Lemkin

Edwin Herbert Lemkin was born March 2, 1921 in Jersey City, NJ. He graduated from the University of Wisconsin with a B.A. in Economics. He became a teacher and taught American History at the high school and college level. He was married on August 30, 1944 to Rosali Sampson. They produced two children. His son Edwin is currently the Under-Secretary of the Air Force for International Affairs. As of 2006, Edwin is retired at Palm Beach Gardens, FL.

Ensign Edwin H. Lemkin

LCS(S) Rocket Boat Crew with their Ensign, Edwin H. Lemkin, Francis Zahn; Coxswain—Edwin R. Williams S2c, M.D. Smithingell Aubert B. Windley Jr.; S2c, S.F. Buchanan, Gunner; George Hamarich Jr., Gunner

The following LCS(S) Rocket Boat Summary was given by Edwin H. Lemkin at Normandy, at the 50th Anniversary of D-Day. His tour group was traveling by bus from battlefield to battlefield. He took over the microphone and visualized June 6, 1944 and began reminiscing to his listeners on board, and the following recording of his D-Day events now lives on forever.

My lecture at Normandy Beach at the 50th Anniversary, while on a sightseeing bus.
The Untold Story of the Rocket Boats
Lieutenant Edwin H. Lemkin, U.S. Navy. Adapted from oral history transcript

I went through Little Creek, VA (an amphibious training center), and as an ensign, I was taken up to Solomons Island, MD, where we became the first rocket boat group. We had thirty-six of us at the beginning and the highest ranking officer was an ensign, that's how new it was.

The rocket boats [LCS(S)] were approximately thirty-six feet long. We had an ensign and a crew of six on each one. We carried forty-eight rockets in racks. We also carried our main batteries amidships, which were twin .50-caliber machine guns, and we had a .30-caliber on the stern.

We crossed the Atlantic on an LST by means of a five-week convoy up to Iceland, all the way over to England. We disembarked from the LST in Wales and were taken by train to Plymouth. We stayed at Plymouth quite a while, training until our boat arrived.

After that, we patrolled the channel, guarding small convoys up and down the English Channel, including a short stint at Slapton Sands. We were at the far reaches of the exercise (Exercise Tiger) and never knew anything about it until many years after.

Before the invasion, we were sent back to Weymouth, and from there we were loaded aboard an LST and dropped off on D-Day, about five miles off the beach. Then we were attached to the scouts and raiders, who had gone in the previous night in boats like ours and in small, inflatable boats, to help the UDT (underwater demolition teams) disarm the hedgehogs (mined obstacles).

We went in ten minutes before H-Hour. Right behind us were the amphibious tanks—unfortunately we know what happened to them. I think only one reached the beach. We fired our rockets about fifty yards off the beach. Our fire control was not accurate, but I guess we made a lot of noise anyway.

Fire directed by a destroyer also hit us and put a big hole in our bow. We kept the boat going for several days and reported to the beachmaster, as directed, and asked him what we should do. He told us to pick up bodies. We picked up some and then we didn't know what to do with them. He said to bring them to the yellow zone. We went to the yellow zone, but they didn't want the bodies, so we put them back in the water.

After several days we sank. I had a .50-caliber ammunition chest aboard filled with silk stockings, perfume, lipstick, and chocolate bars, anticipating a great welcome from the French ladies. When my boat went down, I lost that ammunition chest. It was probably my greatest loss in the war. This has still been a cause of laughter for the last fifty years among the few people who knew about it.

My crew was taken off by one boat, and I was taken off by another ship and eventually assigned, along with those American officers and crews who had lost their boats, to Juno and Gold beaches. We reported to the *George W. Woodward,* headquarters ship for Americans serving with the British assault forces. We were on the British beach for several weeks, helping with their small boat operations. A lone German would come over almost every night and try to drop a few bombs. It was sort of a last gasp of their part.

Eventually, I shipped back to the states. I would say this as far as Normandy is concerned: I am the last one that I know that is alive who was in that operation. I have never found any sign of anybody else. We had approximately twenty-one rocket boats on that beach and every one was sunk, as far as I know, and I don't think there is anybody else living. So, I only give this little report because there is no one else to do it, as far as I know. I eventually ended up as executive officer on an LSM, hit every island in the Pacific, and ended up in Japan. The war was quite an interesting experience.

Ensign Robert A. Cannon

Robert A. Cannon was born on November 11, 1920 in Arlington, MA. He graduated from Boston College in 1943 with a degree in Economics. Upon graduation he went for basic training and OCS. He married my mother, Virginia Noy, on December 28, 1943. They had two sons: Robert F. Cannon, born on February 5, 1947, and Stephen K. Cannon. My dad retired in 1980. After the war, he worked in finance in Boston and later in New Haven, CT. He had nineteen wonderful years of retirement until he passed away on February 23, 1999. He never spoke much about the war. I do remember him always watching *Victory At Sea*. How appropriate! My mom Virginia Cannon retained and donated all my father's pictures of him and his crewmates in hope that they would one day enhance her husbands rocket boat story at Omaha Beach if it were ever told.

Son Robert F. Cannon

Me and My LCS(S) Rocket Boat Crew:
Ray Silak, coxswain; John Walsh, motormac; Walt Mickiewicz, S1c; Carlos Solar, S2c; Francis Pilarcek, S2c; Ed Zarzynski, S1c

Ensign Nicholas J. Zuras

Nicholas Zuras was born on July 9, 1918 in Washington D.C. He graduated East Carolina University in 1943 with a double major in Education and History. He was a high school history teacher for seven years, but went on to become a sales representative for Seagram's in the Washington D.C. area, concentrating on hotels and restaurants. He married Mary Mandis in 1950. They had two children, girls. As of the printing of this book, he resides in Annapolis, MD. He wrote his entire LCS(S) Rocket Boat Story at Omaha Beach and included Ensign Robert A. Cannon, who provided many pictures for this book, but never wrote his story. Since Robert A. Cannon had pictures of his crew in battle, I will include these with Ensign Nicholas Zuras' summary at Omaha Beach, which follows.

LCS(S) Rocket Boat Events, As I Remember Them

LCS(S) Rocket Boat Training, Atlantic Convoy to England, February 1944
Omaha Beach, D-Day, June 6, 1944; Invasion of Northern France
Nicholas J. Zuras
9/10/2006

After a long, difficult, and hazardous trip across the North Atlantic, during the heart of winter, February and March 1944, our convoy reached Plymouth, England without any harm. During the trip across, I had been OOD (Officer on Duty) watches on the Supercon, standing eight feet above the ship's con in heavy foul weather, gear pitching and heaving—holding [on for] dear life—having Corvettes; English Destroyers racing by, sounding their loud horn alarms, alerting us that German subs were in the area.

Ensign Nicholas J. Zuras OOD on LST282 with Ensign Herman F. Vorel
Picture provided by Ensign Robert A. Cannon

English Corvette—Sub-Chaser; HMS Davies

Ensigns, L/R: Robert Canon; Herman Vorel; Edwin H. Lemkin; Nicholas J. Zuras
Picture provided by Nick Zuras

When we finally reached England, we were sent to Vicarage Barracks outside Plymouth, where there was a large pool of LCS(S) Rocket Boat officers and crews. It was at Vicarage Barracks that we were finally exposed to the war. Every evening, the German bombers came over trying to take out a very high and narrow bridge spanning the river. We were ordered to take cover. It was about this time that Ensign Herman F. Vorel and Robert A. Cannon told me that Ensign Peter J. Lojko and Edwin H. Lemkin knew someone at the Command Headquarters in Plymouth that may help us get our orders to leave.

Preparations for D-Day

It was about the third week when orders went out that all assault officers were to report to a briefing. It was in Quonset Hut. Reporting there were LCS(S) officers, DD tank officers, and Rangers Demolition officers.

LCS(S) Officers at Quonset Hut
Identified
Back left: Ensign Richard F. Omeara
Back center: Ensign Maxim Soulier
Back, 2nd from right: Ensign Clement Halupka
Front left: Robert Cannon, piggy back
Head down: Ensign Nicholas J. Zuras
Right: Ltjg. Charles S. Reder
Right, squatting: Ensign Roscoe C. DuMond
Picture provided by Ensign Robert A. Cannon

Underwater Demolition Team in England just prior to D-Day—all unidentified
Picture provided by Ensign Robert A. Cannon

DD-Sherman Tanks approaching Beach (left); Utah Beach was successful (right); but Omaha Beach, most DD-tanks sunk with their crews

In the front part of the Quonset Hut was a layout of the entire Omaha Beach pillboxes, gun placements, houses, etc., and the entire beach with obstacles. They told us about the teller mines on the hedgehogs and obstacles of all kinds. The pillboxes had 88's that had every perimeter on the beach covered.

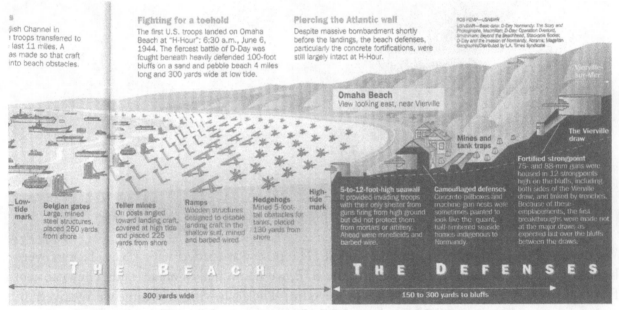

LCS(S) Rocket Boat officer briefing at Quonset Hut and what they observed;
Similar 1994 U.S. World News picture of the Omaha Beach Obstacles and fortification

Asking questions, I remember the English DDT questioning the launching of the American DDT tanks as being too far from the beach—an assumption that would unfortunately come true; that the English DDTs were being launched much closer. The Army DDT tank officers said that they would be okay.

DD Tanks were amphibious swimming tanks. The DD comes from duplex drive, referring to the combination of their normal tracks and propellers. The DD tanks all disembarked from over two miles out, all five beaches. The English tanks suffered low losses. Four of 32 DD tanks sunk at Utah Beach. Most of the 20 plus DD tanks sent into Omaha sank, because they were drawn south of their beach landing mark, when they turned their craft 45 degrees, they were sideways, and the waves sunk them.

DD Sherman tank with its flotation screen lowered

The demo unit was set two hours before the first wave, which was set at 6:30 a.m.; the LCS(S) Rocket Boats at 6 a.m. The fleet was to open fire (bombarding the beach 40 some minutes before H-Hour). We were told that the tide came in at six feet an hour, so that there wasn't very much time that these obstacles were above water. We then were given orders to motor to Portland and board ship. I don't remember the particulars of those orders. I remember I had orders to board LST 375.

We motored to Portland without an incident. The port was loaded with LSTs. Troops were boarding them. The night after boarding the 375, we had a hell of an air raid. They came in from all over, but surprisingly, few LSTs were hit. The following morning we received an order to put gun stops on all 20-mm's on LSTs. The captain of the 375 was Lieutenant Buck, who said that the 20-mm's were strafing other LSTs as the planes flew between them.

D-Day, June 6, 1944

The order to move was given. I was up on the bridge, wondering what we were about to do, noticing the size of the sea. The seas were huge. The seas were coming over the bow heavy. Sometime later we were told to change course. On the 6th of June, the LST 375 anchored off Normandy in heavy seas. At 4:00 a.m. the LCS(S) were told to board their boats on the davits. We were lowered into the water.

LCS(S) Rocket Boats of the USS Bayfield; Picture provided by Albert Kiel, Motormac

The night before, the LCS(S) officers were given a folder marked SECRET. Our orders: the entire map of Omaha Beach, the course to take to the rendezvous area, then to be met by a sub-chaser to guide us to the line of departure that headed us to Red-Green Beach.

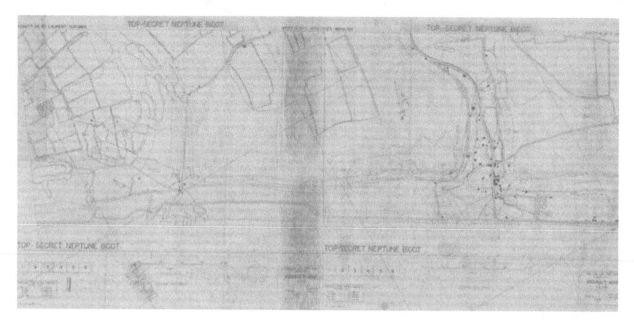

Heading toward the rendezvous, the seas were heavy. Reaching the area, we proceeded to circle, waiting for the escort. Every turn toward the wind we were soaked by heavy spray. I wondered how in the hell we could launch rockets in these kinds of seas. Luckily, the Gray Marine diesel engine was doing the job, pumping out of six inches of water around our feet. The sub-chaser (control vessel) finally showed and we were told to single file toward the beach. Below is a similar plan (diagram) as to how we were to set up from the bottom up. Transports to LCS(S) rendezvous area, LCS(S)'s follow the control vessel, to the line of departure toward Omaha or Utah.

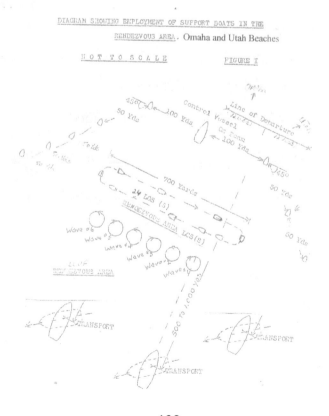

DIAGRAM SHOWING EMPLOYMENT OF SUPPORT BOATS IN THE
RENDEZVOUS AREA. Omaha and Utah Beaches

NOT TO SCALE   FIGURE I

This was the LCS(S) deployment plan given to Ltjg. Charles S. Reder one year earlier for the Invasion of Sicily. It was based on Force General Order No. 1–43, Chapter XV–Annex Sugar, LCS(S). This was the standard Rocket Boat training protocol given to all Rocket Boat officers.

This is a simulation of Omaha and Utah that has been modified by Ensign Ralph Frede's information, who noted in his war highlights that 12 boats went into Utah, 12 into Omaha. Thus, this is a simulation of what occurred.

In seas at our stern, it was difficult to keep the boat on a straight course. Suddenly, the fleet opened up. There were heavy loud guns over our heads. In about 40 minutes it stopped. Suddenly, bombers came over, heading toward the beach.

OPEN FIRE! The big guns of the battleship U.S.S. *Nevada* pound the shore in the early-morning hours of June 6. Although the ship bombardment was far more accurate than Allied bombs, the German bunkers on the coast were so thick that many survived direct hits

I thought, why did they need our rockets? Then the boat's motor began heating up just as our escort ordered us to form a line abreast heading toward the beach.

We kept hoping the extra water we poured into the motor would help. We finally had to pull over to Cannon's boat for more water.

Simulated Ensign Nick Zura's pulling alongside
Ensign Robert Cannon's boat for water during Omaha Beach run

The view ahead was heavy in smoke and clouds of dust. [At] about 300 yards, we began firing the rockets: twelve rockets in each salvo; another salvo about 200 yards. Rockets tumbling (falling) around us—friendly fire. The motor was smoking. I decided to get the hell out of there.

Rockets falling all around us

As I turned, I saw Cannon's boat smoking on the bow. He was hit. He heads away from the beach. I wondered, what he can do? We head toward the 375 when we see the first wave heading toward the beach in very heavy seas. We began seeing German shell fire. The ramps on the LCVPs were hitting heavy seas. The DD tanks were half out of the water, sinking. Some rocket boats are picking up crews off the DDTs. Some DDT crews are in the water.

Then, after all of this, we saw those large Rino barges loaded with Red Cross trucks and heavy equipment under heavy German fire. Again, I questioned why they weren't being told to stand off. Our rocket boat engine is smoking. We continued to head toward where we think the 375 is located. We find her and I begin lowering the rest of the 12 rockets over the side. I figure the firing pins were not set, so no damage could be done.

This was the end of our D-Day Mission at Omaha Beach.

LST-374 LCS(s) "After Action Report" of her 4 Rocket Boats at Omaha Beach; D-DAY

New substantive documentation from my June, 2020 visit to the Navy Archives in College Park Maryland, produced the "After Action Report" by R.B. Hunt of the results of the four Rocket Boat Officers deployed by LST 374 at Omaha Beach, D-Day

In the next 5 sub pages of LST 374 After Action Report, please find the following new and substantive verifications of previous and other Rocket Boat Officer and crew members claims bracketed.

(I) Cover letter by Officer R.B. Hunt of "Secret Letter of LST 374 results Omaha Beach D-Day".

(II) List of all transports that supplied the 12 Rocket Boats of Omaha Beach. The are LST 374 -4, LST 6 – 3, LST 376 – 3 and USS Henrico – 1, USS Samuel Chase -1. This corroborates page 58 line 4 summary by Ensign Ralph E Frede at Utah Beach that 12 Rocket Boats went into Omaha and 12 into Utah Beach D-Day.

(III) Summary of results of LST 374 four Rocket Boat Officers Lt. (jg) William J. Eisemann, Lt. (jg) Albert E. Penalosa, Lt. (jg) William J. File and Lt. (jg) Wesley S. Wallace. This corroborates that all 24 Rocket Boats of Omaha and Utah Beaches had 24 Rockets in the racks and 24 in hull and attempted to shoot all 48 with a few misfires.

(IV) Signatures of all 4 above listed LST 374 Rocket Boat Officers of their paragraph summaries of their results at Omaha Beach D-Day.

Please refer
to file: A16-3(05/Hr)

Serial: 0 3718

UNITED STATES FLEET

LANDING CRAFT AND BASES
EUROPE

5 AUG 1944

SECRET

From: Commander, Amphibious Bases, United Kingdom.
To: Commander, ELEVENTH Amphibious Force.

Subject: Report of Participation in Operation ████

Enclosure: [(A) Secret ltr. From LCS(S) Officers Carried on LST] 1
            374 in Operation ████ of 10 July 1944,
            (unaddressed) on the above subject.

1.   Enclosure (A) is forwarded herewith for information.

R. B. HUNT
By direction

AUG 5 P.M.

84846   8 1497

A163

10 July 1944

From: LCS (S) Officers Carried on LST 374 in
          Operation ███████

To:

Subject: Report of Participation in Operation
          ███████

[1.   The four LCS (S) 's carried aboard LST 374
in Operation ███████ were put in the water in the Transport
Area at approximately H- 210 and proceeded immediately to
Rendezvous Point KL, arriving at about H- 190. They were
the first LCS (S) 's at the Rendezvous Area, being joined
shortly thereafter by three from LST 6, three from LST 376
and one each from the USS HENRICO and the USS SAMUEL CHASE.]   2

     2.   At approximately H- 160 subject LCS (S) 's
received a verbal message presumably from Lt.(jg) ANDREASEN,
Officer-in-Charge, that all would assemble around the buoy at
point KL and leave from there. Subject LCS (S) 's proceeded
immediately to the buoy in question and stood-by there to
await a signal to leave but received none.

     3.   At approximately H- 135 it was discovered that
in the poor visibility and the heavy sea part of the boats had
left. Thereupon the remaining eight LCS (S) 's led by Lt.(jg)
FILE, started for the 6,000 yard line proceeding at full
speed.

     4.   Subject LCS (S) 's arrived at the 6,000 yard
line at H- 45 and found the LCT (DD)'s in the process of
launching their DD tanks; subject LCS (S) 's immediately
assumed position in front of their respective LCT (DD)'s
and proceeded at reduced speed toward the beach followed
by the DD's that survived the launching.

     5.   At approximately H- 15 minutes subject LCS (S)'s
commenced firing HE rockets in accordance with the Operation's
Order with the following results:

8 1437

Subject: Report of Participation in Operation

- -

5-(a)   Lt.(jg) FILE: Fired one ranging shot which was observed to fall on the beach about 200 yards above the water's edge. Thereupon fired 43 additional rockets, two at a time, reloading top 6 rails as necessary, proceeding at slow speed toward the beach throughout the firing period. All rockets hit well up on the beach but the fall of the one's fired toward the last was obcured by smoke and dust from the bombardment in progress.

Total rockets hitting the beach - 44, misfires - 4.

5-(b)   Lt.(jg) EISEMANN: Fired 48 rockets, two at a time in same manner as above. All rockets hit well upon the beach, but fall of latter half was obscured by smoke and dust.

Total rockets hitting beach - 48, misfired - 0.

5-(c)   Lt.(jg) PENALOSA: Fired two ranging shots. First one hit at edge of beach; second hit well up on beach; Fired 44 additonal rockets in same manner as detailed in paragraph 5-(a). All these rockets hit well up on the beach, but fall of majority could not be observed because of smoke and dust.

Total rockets hitting beach - 46, misfires - 2.

5-(d)   Lt.(jg) WALLACE: Fired one ranging shot, which hit at least 200 yards above water's edge. Fired 47 additional rockets in same manner as detailed in paragraph 5-(a), all hitting high up on the beach, but with observation obscured by smoke and dust.

Total rockets hitting the beach - 48, misfires - 0.

6.   At the conclusion of the rocket fire, Lt.(jg) PENALOSA and Lt.(jg) EISEMANN, picked up three DD-tank survivors each and Lt.(jg) WALLACE picked up one DD-tank survivor. All subject LCS (S)'s then returned to the vicinity of the 2,000 yard line where they remained until about H-pluse 90, when they reported to the Deputy Assault Force Commander, and carried out various assigned tasks throughout D-Day.

3

Subject: Report of Participation in Operation

- -

7.   Subject LCS (S)'s remained in the Omaha area until ordered to leave on D plus 18, with the following exceptions:

Lt.(jg) FILE: Made one roundtrip under orders to Portland aboard LST 375, for necessary repairs.

Lt.'s (jg) PENALOSA and EISEMANN: Made one round trip under orders to Southampton aboard LST 374 for necessary repairs.

8.   Throughout most of the period from D-Day to D plus 18 day, subject LCS (S)'s operated for Shuttle Control from HMS Ceres.

9.   On D plus 16 and D plus 17, subject LCS (S)'s were lost in the storm off Omaha Beach. On D plus 18 the officers and crews were ordered by Captain W.M. PERCYFIELD, USN, to report to COUSNAAB, Weymouth, Dorset.

4

WILLIAM H. FILE, Jr.
Lt.(jg) USNR

WILLIAM J. EISEMANN
Lt.(jg) USNR

ALBERT E. PENALOSA
Lt.(jg) USNR

WESLEY S. WALLACE
Lt.(jg) USNR

8 1497

CHAPTER 9

D-Day
Anvil/Dragoon
August 15, 1944

Ensign Peter J. Lojko
Commendation
Southern France

Ensign Albert M. Low
Silver Star Recipient
Purple Heart Recipient

Last Major Deployment of the LCS(S) Rocket Boats
in the European Theatre
as witnessed by

Ens. Leslie H. Dause   Ens. Nicholas J. Zuras   Ens. Roscoe DuMond

Southern France
August 15th 1944
Introduction

Operation Dragoon
From Wikipedia, the free encyclopedia
Operation Dragoon was the Allied invasion of Southern France, on 15 August 1944, as part of World War II. The invasion took place between Toulon and Cannes.

Contents
1. Planning
2. The landings
3. After the landings
4. Notes
5. External links

Planning
During the planning stages, the operation was known as *Anvil*, to complement *Operation Hammer*, which was at that time the codename for the invasion of Normandy. Subsequently both plans were renamed, the latter becoming Operation Overlord, the former becoming Operation *Dragoon;* a name many thought was picked by Winston Churchill, who was opposed to the plan, and claimed to having been "dragooned" into accepting it. (This later turned out not to be true.)

Operation Dragoon
Part of World War II

A map of the operation.

Date	15 August 1944–September 1944
Location	Southern France
Result	Decisive Allied victory

Combatants

United States[1]   Germany

Free France,
United Kingdom

Commanders

Jacob L. Devers   Johannes Blaskowitz

Strength

250,000 (approx)   230,000 (approx)

Casualties

4,500 American, 4,500+   125,000+ (approx)
French

Western European Campaign

Normandy - **Dragoon** - Siegfried Line - Ardennes
Offensive - Elbe

Churchill argued that Operation *Dragoon* diverted resources that would have been put to better use in an invasion of the oil producing regions of the Balkans and then possibly to other Eastern European countries. In addition to further limiting Germany's access to much needed oil, it would also have better positioned the West for the "peace" following World War II by "liberating" these areas from the German occupation and forestalling the Red Army.

The plan originally envisaged a mixture of Free French and American troops taking Toulon and later Marseille, with subsequent revisions encompassing Saint Tropez. The plan was revised throughout 1944, however, with conflict developing between British military staff—who were opposed to the landings, arguing that the troops and equipment should be either retained in Italy or sent there—and American military staff, who were in favor of the assault. This was part of a larger Anglo-American strategic disagreement.

The balance was tipped in favor of *Dragoon* by two events: the eventual fall of Rome in early June, plus the success of Operation Cobra, the breakout from the Normandy pocket, at the end of the month. Operation *Dragoon*'s D-Day was set for 15 August 1944. The final go-ahead was given at short notice.

The U.S. 6th Army Group, also known as the Southern Group of Armies and as Dragoon Force, commanded by Lieutenant General Jacob L. Devers was created in Corsica and activated on August 1, 1944 to consolidate the combined French and American forces that were planning to invade Southern France in Operation *Dragoon*. At first it was subordinate to AFHQ (Allied Forces Headquarters) under the command of Field Marshal Sir Henry Maitland Wilson, who was the supreme commander of the Mediterranean Theater. One month after the invasion, command was handed over to SHAEF (Supreme Headquarters, Allied Expeditionary Forces) under U.S. General Dwight D. Eisenhower, the supreme commander of Allied forces on the Western Front.

The landings
The assault troops were formed of three American Divisions of the VI Corps, reinforced with a French armored division. The 3rd Infantry Division landed on the left at Alpha Beach (Cav-

Monument to the landings of Allied troops under General Patch on the beach of St Tropez, France.

alaire-sur-Mer), the 45th Infantry Division landed in the centre at Delta Beach (Saint Tropez), and the 36th Infantry Division landed on the right at Camel Beach (Saint-Raphaël). At Cap Negre, on the western flank of the main invasion, a large group of French commandos landed to destroy German artillery emplacements (Operation Romeo). These were supported by other French commando groups landing on both flanks, and by Rugby Force, a parachute assault in the LeMuy-Le Luc area by the 1st Airborne Task Force: British 2nd Independent Parachute Brigade, the U.S. 517th Parachute Regimental Combat Team, and a composite U.S. airborne glider regimental combat team formed from the 509th Parachute Infantry Battalion, the 550th Glider Infantry Battalion, and the 1st Battalion, 551st Parachute Infantry Regiment (Operation Dove). The 1st Special Service Force took two offshore islands to protect the beachhead (Operation Sitka). Operation Span, a deception plan, was carried out to shield the main invasion.

Naval gunfire from Allied ships, including the French battleship *Lorraine,* British battleship HMS *Ramillies,* and the American capital ships USS *Texas, Nevada* and *Arkansas.* and a fleet of over 50 cruisers and destroyers supported the landings. Seven Allied escort carriers provided air cover.

Over ninety-four thousand troops and eleven thousand vehicles were landed on the first day. A number of German troops had been diverted to fight the Allied forces in Northern France after Operation Overlord and a major attack by French resistance fighters, coordinated by Captain Aaron Bank of the OSS, helped drive the remaining German forces back from the beachhead in advance of the landing. As a result, the Allied forces met little resistance as they moved inland. The quick success of this invasion, with a twenty-mile penetration in twenty-four hours, sparked a major uprising by resistance fighters in Paris.

Follow-up information included U.S. VI Corps HQ, U.S. Seventh Army HQ, French Army B (later redesignated the *French First Arm,* and French I and II Corps, as well as the 51st Evacuation Hospital.

(http://www.rogue-publishing.com/51st/51st_evacuation_hospital_history.html)

After the landings

The rapid retreat of the German Nineteenth Army resulted in swift gains for the Allied forces. The plans had envisaged greater resistance near the landing areas and underestimated transport needs. The consequent need for vehicle fuel outstripped supply and the shortage proved to be a greater impediment to the advance than German resistance. As a result, several German formations escaped into the Vosges and Germany.

The *Dragoon* force met up with southern thrusts from Overlord in mid-September, near Dijon.

A planned benefit of *Dragoon* was the usefulness of the port of Marseilles. The rapid Allied advance after Operation Cobra and *Dragoon* slowed almost to a halt in September 1944 due to a critical lack of supplies, as thousands of tons of supplies were shunted to NW France to compensate for the inadequacies of port facilities and land transport in Northern Europe. Marseilles and the southern French railways were brought back into service despite heavy damage to the Port of Marseilles and its railroad trunk lines. They became a significant supply route for the Allied advance into Germany, providing about a third of the Allied needs.

Ensign Roscoe C. DuMond

Roscoe C. DuMond was born on February 2, 1920 in Yonkers, NY. He graduated from Cornell in 1942, having majored in Hotel Administration. He worked for Stouffers Restaurant & Hotels from 1946 to 1985 as restaurant hotel manager. He married Bernadine Sutton in August of 1943. They had two daughters. Bernadine passed away in July 1952. He again married later in 1953 to Marguerite Stewart. They had three daughters. He is retired in Palm Coast, FL, as of the completion of this book.

Roscoe, of course, was known by other Rocketboatmen as a "Husky" who participated a year earlier in the Invasion of Sicily (Operation Husky). So his two Rocket Boat missions were Sicily, July 1943, and now Southern France, August 1944. On D-Day, June 6, 1944, he was on standby in the Mediterranean, where his LST had engine damage and went to dry-dock in Africa for repair. He provided an original rocket boat invasion map, which follows, showing all towns on the Southern France Coastline and all the American color coded beach anticipated entry points, plus his actual Rocket Boat Orders with his signature.

Ensign Roscoe C. DuMond and LCS(S) Rocket Boat Crew Picture taken in 1945 in the Pacific

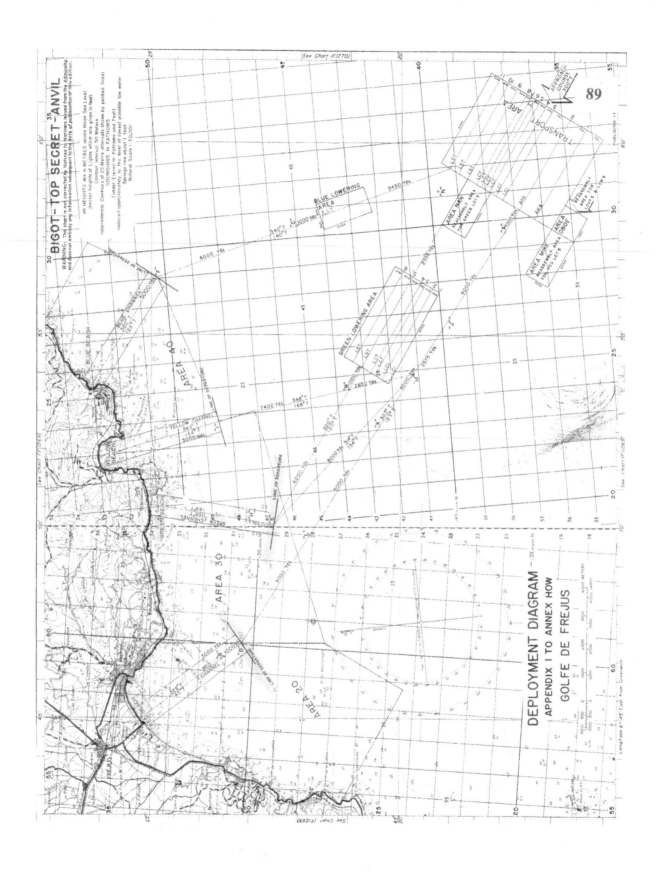

USS Bayfield small boat deployment plan for the Invasion of Southern France (see page 132 where LCS(S) Rocket Boats are then deployed.

U.S.S. BAYFIELD   OPERATION ORDER   AUGUST 1944

1.   Uniform

     Boat Officers and crew will wear impregnated clothing, sheath
knives, steel helmets, gas masks, and kapok lifebelts while landing
with the assault waves. Impregnated clothing and gas mask must be
available for immediate use at all times.

2. LCVP 8 (Ens Vassillaros) when lowered proceed to Green Lowering
Area and report to LCI(L) 76. Stand by that craft until required by
RCT Commander to take him and Headquarters detachment of about 30 men
to land over Green Beach. Upon completion of duty return to BAYFIELD

3. 10 LCVP's divided into pairs, with one officer to each pair, are
assigned as follows:

LST	491	LCVP's 18 & 20	-	Ens CADMUS	-	WAVE 4
LST	501	LCVP's 17 & 19	-	Ens KERN	-	WAVE 9
LST	491	LCVP's 11 & 13	-	Ens WADLEIGH	-	WAVE 11
LST	134	LCVP's 21 & 22	-	Lt(jg)KEFFER	-	WAVE 14
LST	989	LCVP's 12 & 14	-	Ens DALY	-	WAVE 15

These craft will report to their assigned vessel prior to H-140 min
and lie to 200 yards ahead of ramp. As DUKW's are discharged from
LST's they will rendezvous on LCVP's by Waves as follows:

LST	WAVE	NUMBER DUKW
491	4	6
501	9	22
491	11	11
134	14	22
989	15	22

As soon as DUKW Waves are formed, LCVP lead Wave to Reference Vessel
BAKER (PC 546), arriving 15 minutes before time scheduled to leave
for beach. Take position on starboard side of BAKER and lie to. When
dispatched, lead DUKW Waves to Line of Departure for GREEN Beach at
four (4) knots. LCVP manned by Boat Officer guide the formation,
other LCVP's maneuver astern and on the flanks of the formation,
correcting courses of individual DUKW and keeping stragglers closed
up. Leave Line of Departure when dispatched, lead Wave to 1000 yard
marker vessel at four (4) knots and dispatch them to GREEN Beach.

Thereafter LCVP's report to Primary Control Vessel, GREEN Beach
(PC 551) for traffic control and dispatch duty. Wave Commander will
fly numeral flags to indicate number of the Wave.

Page 1 of 4

LANDING DIAGRAM   -   TIMES   -   GREEN BEACH

WAVE NO.	CRAFT	LEAVE BAKER	LEAVE EASY	LANDS AT	
4	6 DUKW	H - 71	H - 26	H + 12	D D D ⌄ D D D
9	22 DUKW	H - 3	H + 42	H + 80	D D D D D D D D D D D D / D D D D D D D D D / D
11	11 DUKW	H + 17	H + 62	H + 100	D D D D D D D D D D D
14	22 DUKW	H + 60	H + 105	H + 143	D D D D D D D D D D D D / D D D D D D D D D / D
15	22 DUKW	H + 70	H + 115	H + 153	D D D D D D D D D D D D / D D D D D D D D D / D

D - DUKW
⌄ - LCVP

4. Green Beach   -   REFERENCE VESSELS -

        BAKER Reference Vessel   -   PC 546
        EASY Reference Vessel   -   SC 1043 prior to H-hour
        HOW   Reference Vessel   -   SC 1043 after H-hour
      - PRIMARY Control Vessel   -   PC 551   stationed at
            reference point EASY, marking the Line o f Departure

    Course from BAKER (PC 546, to EASY (PC 551): 300°T (6000 yds)
    Course from EASY (PC 551) to BEACH - - - : 008°T (5000 yds)
  - There is a VARIATION of 6° WEST

Page 2 of 4

5. <u>Mine Sweepers</u>

Mine Sweepers will lay black and yellow checkered buoys at 1000-yard intervals to a point one mile from BEACH, starting at Line of Departure. B.M.S. will lay OBOE flags on the flank of swept channel to 500 yards of BEACH. These flags will be about 800 yards apart.

6. <u>LCS(S)'s</u> - Scout - BAYFIELD - Lt(jg) TRIPSON - LCS(S) 10 -

BAYFIELD lower LCS(S) Scout on arrival. LCS(S) Scout stand by at BAYFIELD to deliver orders as to Z-hour and BEACH to be assaulte to RED Primary Control, Reference Vessel ABLE, and to RED Sweeper Control at Point MIKE. On arrival at Point MIKE transfer one Scout Officer to RED Sweeper Control.

<u>If RED Beach Is Selected:</u>

LCS(S) Scout follow B.M.S. formation. If RED Sweeper Control becomes a casualty, take station to lead B.M.S. Continue in formation to a point 1000 yards off the center of the Beach. Stop, maintain station, act as Marker Vessel for APEX boats and other pre-assault units until relieved by LCC 22669 at about Z-hour. Then assist LCC in performing its Traffic Control functions, until the Beachmaster is established ashore. When the Beachmaster is ashore, report to him for hydrographic survey and channel marking duty.

or green

<u>If YELLOW Beach is Selected:</u>

RED Sweeper Control transfer Scout Officer to BAYFIELD. Scout accompany NIGHTINGALE's LCC to Line of Departure; then proceed at full speed to a point 1000 yards from center of Beach selected. Take station to mark the Beach for later Waves, until relieved by LCC 22669. Then assist LCC in performing its Traffic Control functions until the Beachmaster is ashore. When Beachmaster is established report to him for hydrographic survey and channel marking duty.

7. LCS(S) ROCKET BOATS   Lt(jg) R.C.DuMOND   - LCS(S) 15
                          Ens   E.J.REYNOLDS - LCS(S) 9
                          Ens   R.G.REYNOLDS - LCS(S) 16

BAYFIELD lower LCS(S)'s in time to have them form rendezvous circle inshore of Reference Vessel ABLE 15 minutes before scheduled to leave for the Beach. (Scheduled to leave ABLE-RED : Z-114).
("   "   "   ABLE-GREEN:Z- 91).
("   "   "   ABLE-YELLOW: Z-102).

Primary Control Vessel leave ABLE at scheduled time. Proceed at six (6) knots, leading LCS(S), Wave ONE and LCT(R) - LCF Wave to the Line of Departure in that order. On arrival at the Line of Departure relieve SC 1030, Reference Vessel. Primary Control Vessel, PC 627 remain on station at Reference Point, marking the Line of Departure for all craft. Dispatch all Waves to the Beach using standard flag

Page 3 of 4

hoists to display flag ZERO followed by a square red flag as identification. For identification paint a broad red horizontal band around stack.

SC 1030 get underway when dispatched by Primary Control. Lead LCS(S) and Wave ONE to Reference Point GEORGE, HOW or OBOE, as appropriate at nine (9) knots. OBOE is 1000 yards inshore of ITEM. On arrival, drop out of formation, maintain station and make this Reference Point for later Waves.

From the Line of Departure to the BEACH LCS(S) proceed in line abreast with the three LCS(S)'s from BAYFIELD on the right and the other three LCS(S)'s from transports named in order from right to left as follows: CARROLL, JEFFERSON, NIGHTINGALE, Wave Commander from BAYFIELD.

SC 1030 stops 4000 yards from BEACH.

Discharge barrage on RED BEACH at Z-4 when 1000 yards off shore.

<u>Fire On GREEN or YELLOW BEACH Only On Specific Orders To Do So</u>

Fire on section of the Beach corresponding to own position in the formation. LCS(S) continue toward the Beach, supporting FIRST Wave with gunfire. Then maneuver about 500 yards off shore, keeping clear of the boat lanes. Engage targets of opportunity on the flanks of the Beaches. At Z ≠ 30 minutes report to LCC 22669 for Traffic Control duty. Remain on assigned flanks of LCC.

Upon receipt of signal QUEEN QUEEN from LCC or PC 627, meaning "Make Smoke", the three LCS(S)'s on the downwind flank proceed immediately, lay smoke on the downwind flank outside the boat lane. The signal QUEEN QUEEN will be made on signal searchlight aimed toward the craft that are to make smoke, when ordered by the Assault Group Commander. When smoking, lay floats at 100-yard intervals and burn pots, maneuvering to maintain the screen. The signal to "Cease Smoke" is NAN NAN.

Prior to dusk on D-day, LCS(S) from BAYFIELD and APA's report to parent ship, when released by Commander RED Assault Group.

LCS(S) APPROACH SCHEDULE FOR APPROPRIATE BEACH

	Lv ABLE	Lv MIKE	Lv DOG	FIRE	
RED BEACH	Z-114	Z-81	Z-18	Z-4	
	Lv ABLE	Lv MIKE	Lv EASY	FIRE	
GREEN BEACH	Z-91	Z-58	Z-18	Z-4	
	Lv ABLE	Lv MIKE	Lv BAKER	Lv ITEM	FIRE
YELLOW BEACH	Z-102	Z-69	Z-55	Z-18	Z-4

8. All ship's boats not assigned in this OPERATION ORDER will be manned and ready for immediate use.

9. The Boat Group Commander and Assistant in the LCP(L)'s will see that boats get off on their assignments as laid out in this ORDER and will then remain close aboard the BAYFIELD for use as Dispatch Boats.

At the Invasion of Southern France, we made several runs to the beach and fired our rockets as we escorted the troops while escorting LCVPs with our rocket boats; enemy shrapnel was falling around us. There was return fire from the beach and it splashed on both sides of the boat. Shrapnel from an explosion wounded two members, who later got purple hearts. Somehow, we [could] not find our ship when returning from the beach, and at daybreak, we were all alone in the Mediterranean with nothing in sight, not even land. We had no navigation equipment on board. Finally, we saw a ship in the distance and headed to it, not knowing if enemy or ours. It was ours, and we were taken on board and our wounded men received Purple Hearts. I next ended up in Marseilles, then returned to the states, and eventually returned to the Pacific in 1945 for the invasion of Japan.

Ensign Roscoe C. Dumond

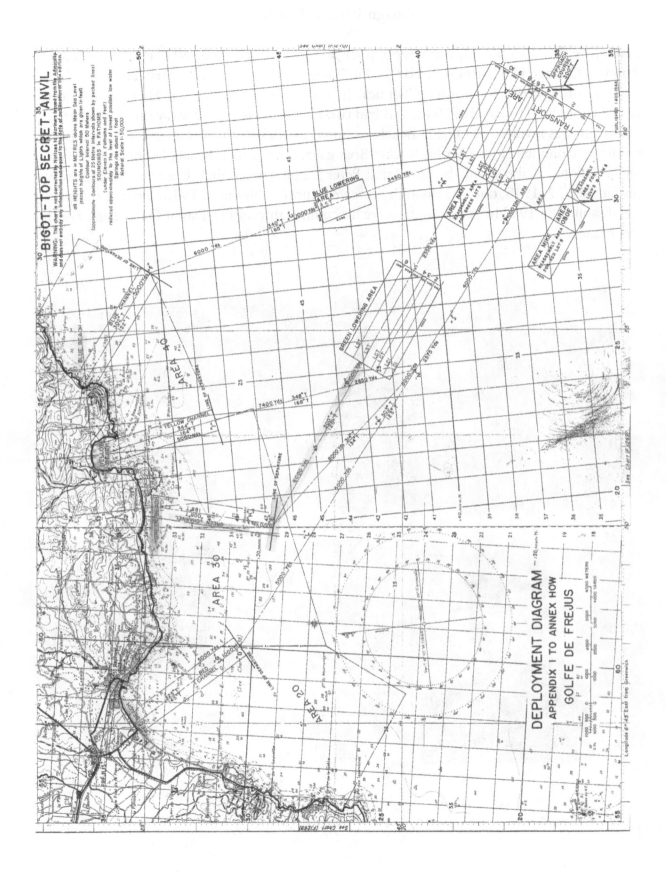

Ensign Peter J. Lojko

Peter Joseph Lojko was born on September 30, 1921 in Nashua, NH. He graduated St. Anselms College in Manchester, NH in 1942 with a degree in Chemistry. He worked the majority of his career for Borden Chemical Incorporated in Purchasing. He was married to Marie Dion on February 10, 1945, and had two children. He passed away on December 13, 1984. He was involved at Omaha Beach, as noted in Nick Zuras' summary, and went on to obtain a "Commendation" for his Rocket Boat gallantry at Green Beach, in Southern France, which follows. It also should be noted that Peter J. Lojko was retired from the Naval Reserve on January 29, 1945, due to a disability received during training in 1943. Despite this physical disability, in 1943 he stayed on to serve his country through D-Day at Omaha and Southern France.

File No. P15
(01/eer)

LST FLOTILLA TEN
c/o Fleet Post Office
New York, New York

21 November 1944

From: Commander LST Flotilla TEN.
To: Ens. Peter LOJKO, USNR

Subject: Commendation for Green Beach Assault Boat Officers.

1.   In accordance with CTG 87.4's letter, P15-00 of 5
September 1944, you are hereby commended:

"For meritorious performance of duty as Assault Boat
Wave and Division Commanders in Green Beach Assault Group, CAMEL Attack
Force, resulting in the sucessful debarkation of assault troops of the
Thirty-Sixth United States Infantry Division on the coast of Southern
France."

The leadership, skillful seamanship, and courage displayed
by these officers in conduction their groups of assault craft through
hazardous waters against the beach under enemy fire, their beaching and
retracting, and their successful return to the appointed rendezvous area,
were in accordance with the highest traditions of the naval service."

W. S. BLAIR, Commander, USNR,
Commander LST Flotilla TEN.

Invasion of Southern France August 17, 1944 and
Memories of Seaman 2c Lawrence P. Berra
by Nicholas J. Zuras
09/10/06

Ensign Nick Zuras   **Larry Berra**

The rocket boat crew and I boarded an LST (don't remember LST number) and headed to North Africa. We passed through the Straits of Gibraltar and entered the Mediterranean, arriving at Bezerte, Tunisia (North Africa). The passage was uneventful, with destroyer escorts doing yeoman's job, keeping German subs off of our tails. After a week at sea we were glad to set foot on dry land.

While in Bezerte, I decided to make a crew change. I went to the port command and requested to release one of the crew. It was done. Two days later, a Seaman First Class came on board by the name of Larry Berra, with a well strapped duffel bag and a catcher's mitt strapped on top. The change was great. He followed orders quickly and well. Larry had an intense desire to have someone play ball with him on the beach whenever possible. We would often find him asking the crew to pitch to him. In one instance, when Churchill's entourage came through the camp at break-neck speed, to observe the readiness of the LSTs for the invasion, he nearly ran Larry over while in a catcher's stance.

On about the end of July, we headed for Naples, Italy. The rocket boat crew and officers were given orders to report to Nieceda, a port north of the Bay of Naples. The port was packed with LSTs. The rocket boat crews and officers were billeted in a huge garage-looking barracks. Boat officer Ensign George Smith and I decided to sleep on the roof with a tent-like cover for a roof. It was hot in July in the Mediterranean. There was no training in rocket boat maneuvers, just sleeping, and on occasion, Smith and I motored over to Capri. It was a great way to fight a war. We also took in the opera, *La Tosca.* Smith knew all about that one. We also did a great deal of recreating at the Crispy House, which was the Naples officers' club. We met Doug Fairbanks in his three stripes. We had a few laughs with Doug. He asked us about our Omaha outing.

This great duty ended on August the 4th, when I received orders to board the USS Barnett APA 5, which I was informed was anchored in the Bay of Naples. Trying to find the Barnett in the Bay of Naples with hundreds of huge ships was very difficult. I located her in the southern part of the bay, with all of the other APAs surrounded by the fleet. We were lifted up on one of her forward davits. I was told by the Exec that the APAs were in a protected setting, surrounded by the fleet for protection against subs. This was my first exposure to the real Navy; that is, the Navy with a whole lot of braid. Those of us officers at this level of duty were not allowed to lift a finger, "so to speak." The mess was "spit and polish," as they say in the fleet. I was seated according to rank. As an ensign, I was low man at that table, but I didn't have to ask for anything; the stewards were on top of every course. They poured my coffee, took my dish, and at one time, I dropped my napkin, and the steward was there. Silverware everywhere. It was nice. The staterooms were large. George Smith and I were in one room, next to the Exec's stateroom.

About the 10th of August, I was ordered to see the Exec's officer, who began to interview me about Normandy (Omaha Beach). He kept asking why I volunteered for duty with the Block Ship Harbor. Whatever I talked about, the more he wanted to know. He wanted to know about the Mulberries and Gooseberries, which were all code names for the operation of the landing after the artificial harbor was installed. I learned later that the APA 5 was in Normandy. I guess he was checking me out for something.

On about the 10th, or a few days before the landing, I was told to report to the Communications officer, who informed me that they were to install a radio on my rocket boat. I was given a series of instructions on its use and that I was only to answer to calls from the APA 5, not to relay any comments on my part during the firing of the rockets or landing of the troops. On the 15th, at 4:00 a.m., we were lowered with 36 rockets, a complete load of 50- and 30-caliber ammo, and given a course. We proceeded toward the beach about five miles off. I can't recall if it was St. Tropez or San Rafael. The weather was great, with smooth seas and no enemy fire, which was different than Omaha, and very welcomed. At 300 yards, I decided to fire the first 12 rockets, six on each rack. The rocket boats we were given for this operation were brand new. The great feature of these boats was that the rocket racks from where the 4.5 rockets were fired were fixed in a trajectory mode, which prevented the racks from falling. If the racks had fallen, the rockets would have penetrated the bow of the boat upon being fired. This happened on Omaha Beach.

USS *LCI(R)-* 763

- Landing Craft, Infantry (Rocket):
- Displacement: 385 tons (full load)
- Length: 160'4"
- Beam: 23'3"
- Draft: 2'8" forward, 5'0" aft (landing)
- Speed: 15.5 knots
- Armament: 1 40mm, 4 20mm, 6 5" rocket launchers
- Complement: 3 officers, 31 enlisted
- 8 GM diesel engines, twin screws

At about 200 yards, we began getting friendly fire. With rockets falling around us from the LST Rockets and LCI Rockets, I decided to fire the second salvo of 12 rockets, and again at 100 yards, the third salvo. At this distance, the beach was very clear, no smoke from the bombardment of the fleet. More tumbling rockets from the LCTs and LCIs, at which point I heard one of the crew in the loading area of the boat yell, "Let's get the hell out of here, Mr. Zuras!" Before turning to port to avoid being hit, one of the crew leaned against the armor plating of the racks and yelled out, because he was burned on his side. Nothing could be done, we had to get out of the range of those tumbling rockets. What amazed the coxswain, the signalman, and I, at the helm, was that there was no enemy fire; it was like a dry run. What was evident was a huge number of dead fish in the water.

As we headed back to the USS Barnett, I began thinking of my brother, Ensign George Zuras, who was a boat officer on APA 69—USS Elizabeth C. Stanton. We had located each other in Naples, and spent time on Capri. Now heading back to the Barnett, I wondered where he was. At about a mile off the beach, I saw his ship. We head toward the Stanton, and with my binoculars, I saw him on a battle station on the ship's bridge in from of the con. I waved and suddenly became aware that his battle station was the most dangerous station during battle. Enemy fighters go for either the stern or the bow to disable a ship. As I waved going by, I yelled for him to get the hell off the bridge. I don't know if he heard me. Since the war, he and I never talk about those days, even the ones on Capri. On returning to the Barnett, we were hauled up on the davit and I was ordered to see the Exec. He briefed me, and we shook hands, with a job well done." Well, there was nothing that happened by enemy fire, so we were lucky. On the 22nd of August, I was put ashore in Marseille, France. I kept my orders, saying, "Performance of duty was in all respects satisfactory"; that came from the real Navy, a four stripper.

Delbert F. Barker
Seaman 2c under
Ensign George F. Smith
Southern France

Southern France
Blue Beach, 6:00 a.m., August 15, 1944

Ensign Leslie H. Dause

Leslie H. Dause was born on January 10, 1917 in Pulaski County, KY. He graduated from Berea College, Berea, KY, in 1943. He obtained a master's degree from the University of Kentucky in 1956. He married Thelma McKinley on October 23, 1943. He was an elementary school principal in Russell Springs, KY. He was also a high school basketball coach. He passed away on October 29, 1974.

Documents and orders obtained in his personal file evidence his participation in the Rocket Boat Program at the Invasion of Southern France, August 15, 1944. The following pages are self-explanatory and a great precursor to Ensign Albert Low, who also went into Blue Beach.

Ensign Leslie H. Dause

Having completed his Solomons, MD, Rocket Boat training course, January 31, 1944, with the first of three groups of 24 Rocket Boat Crews, as noted on page thirty-three, Ensign Dause left Lido Beach, Long Island for his LST Atlantic cruise and ended up at Dartmouth, England by April 18, 1944 with a group of eleven LCS(S) Rocket Boat officers and crews in total, in preparations for D-Day. On June 6, 1944, D-Day, Ensign Dause commanded an LCI carrying troops ashore at Utah Beach. He wrote his wife Thelma stating that he never felt so sorry for anyone as he did for those men he left on the beach. He next participated in LCS(S) Rocket Boat Missions at Southern France, eight weeks later.

```
                        UNITED STATES FLEET
                     ADVANCED AMPHIBIOUS BASE
                     DARTMOUTH, DEVON, U.K.



                                          18 April 1944

        Memorandum to Senior Officer LCS(S) Crews:

        1. The records in the Chief Ships Clerks Office indicate the
        following officers have not turned in their Officer Qualifications
        Questionnaires:

                ATTWOOD, Curtis L.            Ensign, D-V(G)
                GOLDSMITH, Robert Hiram       Ensign, D-V(G)
                HURLEY, Stuart P.             Ensign, D-V(G)
                LOW, Albert M.                Ensign, D-V(G)

        2. It is requested that the above named officers turn in their
        questionnaires as soon as possible.

        3. Records in Office indicate that there are (11) LCS(S) Officers
        attached to the Base as of this date. These officers names are listed
        below. If names are spelled incorrectly, ranks and classifications are
        incorrect, or other information missing it is requested that the officer
        please inform this office.
```

Name	Rank	Date Rank	Active duty date
ATTWOOD, Curtis L.	Ensign, D-V(G), USNR	20 Oct 1943	20 Oct 1943
DAILY, James L.	Ensign, D-V(G), USNR	28 July 1943	28 July 1943
DAUSE, Leslie H.	Ensign, D-V(G), USNR	20 Oct 1943	?
FREDE, Ralph E.	Ensign, D-V(G), USNR	28 Oct 1943	?
GERBER, Morris	Ensign, D-V(G), USNR	?24 Nov	?
GOLDSMITH, Robert H.	Ensign, D-V(G), USNR	21 Jan 1943	17 Feb 1943
HOLMES, Stoke P. Jr.	Ensign, D-V(G), USNR	8 Nov 1943	24 Nov 1943
HURLEY, Stuart P.	Ensign, D-V(G), USNR	29 Oct 1943	29 Oct 1943
LANEY, Lemuel C.	Ensign, D-V(G), USNR	28 Oct 1943	?
LOW, Albert M.	Ensign, D-V(G), USNR	24 Nov 1943	24 Nov 1943
SMITH, Geroge F.	Ensign, D-V(G), USNR	20 Oct 1943	20 Oct 1943

The following two pages include Ensign Dause's hand-sketched Rocket Boat Plan for Blue Beach and actual timeframe orders for rendezvous, departure, commencement of offense Rocket Boat mission at Blue Beach for 6 LCS(S) Rocket Boats.

Ensign Leslie H. Dause

```
         TIMETABLE FOR THE MORNING OF D DAY
(If H-hour is changed, this schedule will change accordingly)

0300 - Up all ship's company, NCDU and NGLO units.

0315 - Breakfast for crew and NCDU crews.

0400 - Breakfast for ship's officers, NGLO and NCDU officers.

0445 - Up all troops.  Up all heads throughout the ship.

0445 - (**) Condition Four.  NCDU and NGLO units man your boats.

0500 - Breakfast for Troops.

0500 - (**) Lower away all NCDU boats, LCSs and LCMs and LCVPs
       #14, #19, #20, ##, #24, #11, and #13.

0530 - Breakfast for troop officers.

0600 - Davit Boat crews may get coffee in crew's mess.  Be on
       station by H-90.

0645 - Boat crews and davit operators prepare to lower.  Launch
       LCVP's #2, #28, and #32 when ready.

0645 - Troops muster by boat teams in your compartments.  Prepare
       to debark.

0700 - First loading group proceed to debarkation stations.

       (Boats to be lowered when loaded and ready)

       (First DICKMAN wave leaves the Rendezvous Area H-10)

0800 - H Hour.

(**) Time approximate, depending upon arrival in Transport Area.
     May be a little earlier.
```

Actual Plan of Debarkation from USS Dickman; D-Day, Southern France, August 15, 1944. LCS(S)'s to be lowered 0500 hrs for Blue Beach.

Ensign Leslie H. Dause's hand-drawn diagram of control boat (1) and 5 LCS(S) Rocket Boats headed for Blue Beach.

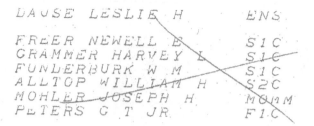

DAUSE LESLIE H   ENS
FREER NEWELL B   S1C
GRAMMER HARVEY L   S1C
FUNDERBURK W M   S1C
ALLTOP WILLIAM H   S2C
MOHLER JOSEPH H   MOMM
PETERS G T JR   F1C

Ensign Leslie Dause's Rocket Boat Crew

Top Secret Bigot Map of Blue Beach Lowering area, rendezvous area, line of departure for LCS(S) Rocket Boats

Ensign Leslie Dause's summary of LCS(S) actions D-Day, Southern France

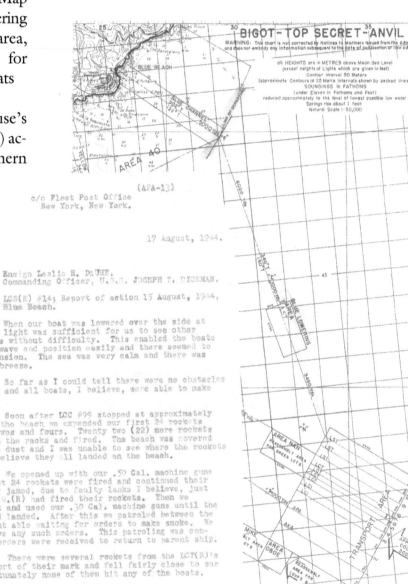

BIGOT - TOP SECRET - ANVIL

WARNING: This chart is not corrected by Notices to Mariners issued from the Admiralty and does not embody any information subsequent to the date of publication of new edition.

all HEIGHTS are in METRES above Mean Sea Level
(except heights of Lights which are given in feet)
Contour Interval 50 Meters
(approximate Contours of 25 Metre intervals shown by pecked lines)
SOUNDINGS in FATHOMS
(under Eleven in Fathoms and Feet)
reduced approximately to the level of lowest possible low water
Springs rise about 1 foot
Natural Scale 1: 50,000

(APA-13)

c/o Fleet Post Office
New York, New York.

17 August, 1944.

From: Ensign Leslie H. DAUSE.
To: Commanding Officer, U.S.S. JOSEPH T. DICKMAN.

Subject: LCS(S) #14; Report of action 15 August, 1944,
            Blue Beach.

1.   When our boat was lowered over the side at about 0510 the light was sufficient for us to see other ships and boats without difficulty. This enabled the boats to find their wave and position easily and there seemed to be little confusion. The sea was very calm and there was only a slight breeze.

2.   So far as I could tell there were no obstacles to small boats and all boats, I believe, were able to make a dry landing.

3.   Soon after LCC #99 stopped at approximately 1200 yds from the beach we expended our first 24 rockets in bursts of twos and fours. Twenty two (22) more rockets were loaded in the racks and fired. The beach was covered with smoke and dust and I was unable to see where the rockets landed but I believe they all landed on the beach.

4.   We opened up with our .50 Cal. machine guns after the first 24 rockets were fired and continued their use until they jammed, due to faulty locks I believe, just after the L.C.M.(R) had fired their rockets. Then we turned to port and used our .30 Cal. machine guns until the first wave had landed. After this we patroled between the beach and point able waiting for orders to make smoke. We did not receive any such orders. This patroling was continued until orders were received to return to parent ship.

5.   There were several rockets from the LCT(R)'s which fell short of their mark and fell fairly close to our boats but fortunately none of them hit any of the boats.

6.   No damage was done to our boat.

7.   I did not see any casualties to troops on our beach.

                        L. H. DAUSE,
                        Ens., U.S.N.R.

Coxswain Newell Freer

I enlisted in the navy at the age of eighteen and went to boot camp in Sampson, NY. Following several weeks of training, I was sent to Little Creek, VA, and then to Solomons, MD, for training in "Rocket Boats."

Our orders were to sail aboard a ship (LST) to Scotland in a large convoy, then to England, and on June 6, 1944, D-Day, to Normandy, France. Our rocket boat on D-Day was transferred to another crew, and our crew was involved in LST related duties landing soldiers and vehicles ashore.

In early August 1944, our crew was transferred to the transport USS Dickman in preparation for the invasion of Southern France. What a majestic ship she was. Immediately we started our review of Rocket Boat maneuvers with our original crew that had trained together eight months earlier in Solomons, MD. Our crew is listed to the right.

Coxswain Newell Freer

I was the coxswain of Ensign Leslie Dause's crew. On the morning of August 15, 1944, we unloaded our boat and proceeded to the rendezvous point on the Bigot map, on preceding page. These Bigot maps were supplied by the French Underground and they were the most updated, detailed maps identifying enemy fortifications. We waited until all the boats convened at the rendezvous point, then proceeded into Blue Beach. My duty as coxswain was to get that boat to the beach safely and timely, an onerous task given the obstacles. On the way in, I spotted a mine. We were not concerned about the ones we could see, because it was easy to avoid them. Only the mines under the water caused us concern.

At about 1,200 yards before the beach, we released our rockets, and when close enough, we strafed the beach with our 50-caliber and 30-caliber machine guns. One of the rocket boats to our right side (I believe the Albert M. Low crew) became involved in a gunfight with a machine gun emplacement on the shore. The boat sustained about 50 bullet holes, but did survive. We got back to the USS Dickman safe and sound as we passed the first wave of soldiers headed into action. This was our last Rocket Boat encounter in 1944.

Joseph H. Mohler
Motormechinist under
Ensign Leslie H. Dause
Southern France

Newell Freer's Rocket Boat (circled) on LST50, hinging on davits in Naples, Italy, 1944

Ensign Albert M. Low

After receiving commendations at Utah Beach for having destroyed 6 objectives which were German machine gun nests, fortified houses and camouflaged 88mm encasements, and also acting as a decoy for battleships to lock onto coordinates of higher up (cliff) embedded fortifications to blow them out, the "Quintessential Rocket Boat Crew" marched onto the Invasion of Southern France with similar alacrity, ardor and results only this time sustaining severe wounds and casualties.

The Quintessential Rocket Boat Crew

L/R – S2c; Thomas J. Dolan
     Ensign; Albert M. Low
     S2c; Clinton E. Birch

MOMM3c; Charles R. Rew Jr.
S1c; William L. Ford
S2c; Jerry J. Bergamo

```
LOW  ALBERT M            ENS        8/4/85
MC CANDLESS C C JR   F1  MOMM221456
BERGAMO JERRY J      S2C     8155316
REW  CHARLES R JR    MOMM3C6055887
DOLAN THOMAS J       S2C     8119026
BIRCH CLINTON E      S2C     6674089
FORD WILLIAM L       S1C     6092425
                          6
```

"Events may belong to history, but heroic performance belong to them that live them. My crew and I feared we die yet such premonitions were seldom vented and we didn't let fear interfere with duty!"
                         Ensign Albert M. Low

USS Dickman unloading small craft for an invasion including an LCS(S) Rocket Boat lower left of picture (perhaps the Albert M. Low crew at Southern France)

Ensign Albert M. Low

15 August 1944. D-Day, Southern France. Combat is theater in grand style; indeed, ultimate style. The Morbid Spirit is on stage with epee-sharp and mal intent. The cast may be cold with fear, but their performance will be compelling. None can be indifferent.

Rocket boat 13 was on that stage; who we were, the crew and I, and who we aspired to become, heroes all, were there too: joined, ready to battle. Under less sanguine circumstances the spectacle might be forgotten; but with the lives of tens of thousands at risk, there would be little chance of forgetting. Events may belong to history, but heroic performances belong to those who live them. My crew and I feared we'd die; yet such premonitions were seldom vented, and we didn't let fear interfere with duty. Our expert in Beaver Creek jargon expressed our battle-ready state of mind when he said, "We'll kick their asses!"

Alongside the ship, with davit hoists disengaged, we went through our customary routine. Sandy started the engine and reported all systems functioning. Raymond reported the diesel "A-okay." MacAndrews signaled satisfaction with his guns. Ruggles and Brown reported all lines in and fenders clear. Confident that the boat was shipshape, I ordered Sanderson to proceed to the floating platform by the Jacob's ladder, where First Lieutenant Hansford Scott and his radioman waited.

"Scotty" took station at my welded seat, claiming the ranking officer's right to choose his battle station. He wasn't familiar with a captain's prerogative. Being too busy to set him straight, I gave up the seat.

Stations manned, all items checked, I conned to the rendezvous area where boats thirteen, fourteen, and fifteen, and Woofus four and five were to join. Per the plan, I took position of the aft port quarter of control boat William.

To our port loomed the great ship USS Texas; aft was the Nevada, ahead was the Philadelphia. Moonglow and lesser light settled luminously on angular masses. Benign imagination re-formed battleships into low-lying islands.

All was going according to schedule except that the Amphibious Coordination Officer (ACO) on control boat William signaled the first wave of soldiers ahead before releasing the support boats. Apparently, he was confused as to which boats were to lead the first wave. I conned to the ACO, hoping to set things right. He waved me off, all the while shouting inappropriate commands.

"Damn," I thought, "I've got to ignore a lieutenant commander's orders or miss the invasion."

I powered past William, assuming position ahead of the first wave. Weeks later, based on a rumored ALNAV*, scuttlebutt was that ACO had been intoxicated that early morning, that he'd since been demoted to lieutenant, and would probably be bypassed for the remainder of his career. If what I'd heard was true, he now had reason enough to drink himself to oblivion.

With the coming of first light, an armada emerged, vast beyond believing. Ships extended from one point of the compass to the other; so many crowded the horizon that comprehension of numbers was impossible. Among the mass were shapes so new that I could neither recognize their class, nor understand their function.

---

*ALNAV: Acronym for All Navy, an all units communication

Our assignment was to direct the initial wave to the landing site, protect it with close gunfire support, then to advance with them as an assault team to widen the bridgehead. NGLO and his radioman were to maintain contact with the most forward platoons, helping us support the invasion with rocket and small arms fire. Orders required that I continue with the assigned Army unit until released by its commander.

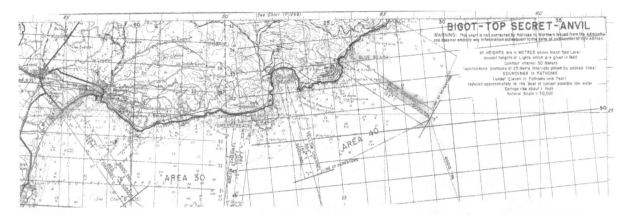

Enemy aircraft from Africa unloaded hundreds of bombs on Blue Beach, reducing landscape to hellscape. Explosions whirred-up and scattered all manner of carnage like shuck before flailing carbines. The flailing was not of wheat, but of outrage; the grim reaper controlled the combines, and his intent was slaughter.

With the squeeze of an anonymous marksman's trigger, NGLO Scott slumped over my coxswain's feet. Sandy looked up at me. We looked at the lieutenant's body. "Doggone," Sanderson said, "He's dead." We pushed him aside. More pressing issues diverted our attention.

Warriors lay on the beach. Some sought cover; those unable to move lay still. I maneuvered close to shore, making the best effort to protect soldiers who had fanned outward from their LCVPs. I fired rockets at real and imagined enemies. My gunners fired at any movement that looked questionable. Most often, enemy positions were well camouflaged, but smoke traces from their lines of fire or from gun barrels were a giveaway.

Projectiles whined toward the fleet. A relative few took aim at us; but even as waterspouts drenched the boat, we were so engaged that we gave little notice. As enemy bullets converged seaward, we sought to saturate the enemy's beach targets. All eight machine guns were in action at one time, as well as six thirty-calibers and MacAndrews' twin fifties. Most often, rockets were also in flight. My hand-held Thompson added its bit. Battlefield haze thickened so densely that we could barely see. Were the Holy Mother on the beach, she'd have been shot.

I had little thought of NGLO's radioman until he appeared by my side. "Sir, they want your help."

"Who?"

"My platoon, Sir. They're calling for help."

"Where?"

"I'm not sure, Sir, but I have radio contact."

"What do they want?"

"They need help, Sir." His eyes said, "You should know. My lieutenant would know."

"Gimme the phone."

"Press the button, Sir," he said, "to talk."

"Ensign Low on Support Boat Thirteen," I said. "Do you read me?"

"Lieutenant Garver here. Loud and strong. Dammit, we need rockets. How about some rockets!"

"Where?"

"Coordinates ...."

"No coordinates."

"Can you see that hotel with the red roof?" he questioned.

"Yes sir."

"See the brown house, about 150 yards beyond it?"

"Yes sir."

"That shithouse is giving us hell. Lay rockets on it."

"How close are your men?"

"About twenty yards, maybe thirty, stopped cold."

"Twenty yards is too close," I shouted, "especially toward the back. Rockets might hit among them."

"We're not in back."

"Twenty yards is awful close."

"Give us ten minutes to dig in."

"Okay. Ten minutes."

I didn't want to fire from straight seaward. Deflection might hit Garver's soldiers. Instead, I plotted a course not quite perpendicular to the beach but in line with the strong point. We executed practice runs a couple of times. Unless the salvo fell far from where it was aimed, Garver's men would be safe.

Ten minutes plus had passed. I advised Lieutenant Garver that we were prepared to fire if he and his crowd were ready.

"I can sequence fire," I replied, "but to keep on target, I've got to lie still in the water. If I do that, the goddamn eighty-eights will kill us!"

"Tough," Garver replied. "Want easy duty? Join us. I've got rifles to spare. The guys who owned them won't complain."

Sarcasm, though bitter to receive, was justified. Compared to infantrymen, we Navy people were on a pleasure boat ride.

"Lieutenant Garver, Sir, let me saturate the bastards with a salvo. The least it will do is raise all the dust you can use."

"Permission granted."

"Thank you, Sir. Rocket boat thirteen over and out."

"Look," I said to the crew, "the problem is that we will be dead in the water. MacAndrews, keep your twin fifties trained on the mortar nests. You've got to keep them down."

MacAndrews grinned a tight grin and pointed his right thumb upwards.

"And you guys," I pointed to Brown and Raymond, "reload fast. Fast! And, for Christ's sake, you guys on the machine guns, keep your heads down."

Within seconds, I'd reset the fuses to explode at contact, a set that would raise the most dust.

"Okay, Sandy? Dead in the water and pointed right-on until we've unloaded four salvos. What do you think?"

"Circle, Sir. Doggone it, Sir, it's the only way."

"What?"

"Circle, Sir. Don't let 'er lay still."

Immediately, I saw the light. Thank God for his opinion. When circling, pitch and roll wouldn't be much of a problem, and we could better defend ourselves. The dirt roused on the first run would hang in the air for the best part of a minute, time enough for us to execute a full turn. We might blind the strong point for five minutes or more, I thought. We paused, probably to pray, then, all stations manned, we started the run.

My ranging shot was nearly perfect. I followed with a four rocket salvo, then kicked Sandy on the right shoulder, to heel the boat to a tight circle. MacAndrews' twin fifties jack-hammered my eardrums, but an ensign's pain succumbed to a captain's thrill of seeing his target clouded. Seconds later, we let go another four rocket salvo, once more with good results. Sandy retraced our wake and, at the instant of line-up, I pressed the "all" button. Rockets took off. Seconds later, and a thousand yards ahead, shock wave and fireball engulfed man and machine.

Retracing our wake, we repeated the attack. Cervone observed smoke puffs issuing from a cut in the hill above the strong point. Examination through binoculars revealed two sets of gun barrels and four, five, maybe six soldiers. These were the defenders whose gunfire had stalled our infantry.

Amply frightened, amply informed, amply motivated, I headed straight to point-blank range, machine guns firing and rockets soaring. The boat jammed into a sandbar, dug a furrow and hung there. Were we unable to power off; we'd soon run out of ammunition and be killed. In the meantime, a firefight between our floating machine gun platform with rockets, and their fixed emplacement, also with machine guns, was joined.

Rockets flew until we had no more but continued the attack with machine guns. The effect appeared murderous.

As clouds lifted and sight lines cleared, lines of splashes converging toward the boat brought to mind memories, during that life when the world knew peace, of how kids sometimes amused themselves by skipping stones across still waters. But these splashes were contrived to kill, not amuse. Fractious sounds excited the air. Bullets tore through the hull and crashed into the cockpit.

A gasp and a cry! Sanderson collapsed; his mouth and nose plastered with blood, his left eye socket empty. The eyeball, dangling from a strand of tissue, wobbled against a blood-soaked cheek. My own warm blood flowed down my leg, saturating sock and shoe. I let go the cowling, lowered into the cockpit and grabbed the helm, yet slippery with gore. Taking a quick bearing, I headed the boat toward open water. Oncoming shots smashed into the smoke pots. Had those pots not been there, most of us would have been killed.

"Should I live through this," I thought, "what stories I'll have to tell."

I dusted sulfa powder into Sandy's wound, tore the eye from its sleeve and threw it overboard. He didn't react, perhaps because of shock.

Within the hour, I'd sidled to a destroyer in search for a medic to take care of my coxswain. My knees buckled as I stepped from my boat to the destroyer's deck, holding him in my arms.

He had to be safe. Strength, mine by virtue of a lifetime of striving for self-pride, wouldn't permit me to let him fall. Through this comrade, I might take membership in the club of those who respect themselves.

I remanded Sanderson to the ship's doctor. As to my wound, heat from the ricochet had cauterized a sterile hole. The ship's doctor removed the bullet, gave me a shot of something, a tin of aspirin, tape, a roll of bandage, and wished me luck.

The destroyer's CO radioed the Dickman that my rocket boat was returning for more ammunition and new coxswain.

In parting, Sanderson joked that he'd be another Popeye. "Taking life easy," he said, "with a pension." I thought he meant it, and that maybe he'd earned it.

Back at the Dickman, sailors lined the ship's rail to get a look at our battle-scarred boat. Meanwhile, my crew cleaned up, mainly by throwing thousands of cartridge shells and connector clips overboard. We were re-supplied with 30- and 50-caliber machine gun cartridges and the remaining rockets in ship's inventory.

A replacement coxswain arrived in the person of Tim McNutt, a sailor who'd thrown a potato that splashed me months earlier. Most likely the assignment was the anti-Semitic Lieutenant Eggar's way of insinuating control. I was anything but pleased.

With the boat fueled, and having taken on ammunition and rations, I gave the coxswain instructions to follow a course midway between the edge of Blue Beach and the coastal gun, as shown on Annex Baker. I avoided the boat lane to save time.

What I took to be the fifth, sixth, and seventh waves were returning to be reloaded and sent out again. Delivery of human and other cargo would continue for weeks. The grinding fields would consume all offerings and cry for more.

McNutt caught on quickly. This coxswain, like Sanderson, had a special feel for boats. To hell with the potato thing, I thought, the kid is good. We'll get along just fine.

We returned to witness a standoff. The enemy had Lieutenant Garver's platoon under defensive fire, and Lieutenant Garver's platoon had them under offensive fire. I joined the attack, hoping to make a difference, but wary of getting hung on a sandbar and being creamed again.

Bullets hit head-on. Neither the crew nor I could figure where the shots were coming from. Well concealed, the attacker raked the boat from stem to stern. Crew hid behind armor. As for me, being on con meant being exposed. After absorbing an uncountable number of hits, Cervone located a machine gun between clumps of trees about six hundred yards away. We fired our guns until their barrels steamed, but to no visible effect. I had two racks of rockets with a range of seven hundred and fifty yards. If I could get close enough to the target, those rockets would lambaste anything, and now was the time to use them.

I got close, the salvo landed dead-on, and the enemy was zilched.

A U.S. tank, its exhaust pipe thrust upward like a cat in heat, joined the attack. "At last," I thought, "exactly what we need, heavily armored land power!" The thought was ruminating through my mind when the tank blew up. Was there no justice?

Another machine gun nest joined the fray. Again, I directed McNutt to within the seven hundred-fifty yard rocket range; instead, the boat reversed course and headed to sea. Thinking that the steering mechanism must have ruptured, I went below to investigate. Incredibly, the coxswain was conning on his own.

"What are you doing, McNutt?"

"I'm going back to the Dickman."

"You're not."

"Yes, Sir, I am."

"Get hold of yourself, McNutt. Turn the boat around and we'll forget this disobedience."

"You're going to kill us, Mr. Low."

"McNutt," I replied, " we've got a job to do, and we're doing it. Now, turn this boat around."

"Sir, you're gonna kill us all. I'm going back to the Dickman. I want to see my officer."

"I'm your officer, McNutt. Turn the boat around."

"Sir, you're gonna kill us all. I'm going back to the Dickman."

I pulled my .45 from its holster and held the bore directly at McNutt's face, maybe an inch from his nose.

"I don't have time to argue. Those soldiers need us, and we're going back. We fight with you alive, or we fight with you dead. Your choice."

A reddish face turned white. The weapon's bore must have looked like a cannon's mouth.

"You wouldn't, Mr. Low!"

"I will."

"You wouldn't, Sir. You wouldn't."

"Get this, McNutt, if you don't obey orders, I've got to."

"You wouldn't, Sir. I know you wouldn't."

I'd taken the wrong approach, but now was into it and had to continue the bluff.

"McNutt, I'm going to count to three. At three, I'm going to pull the trigger. No halves or quarters, it will be one ... two ... three. You won't hear three. I'm starting now. Make up your mind."

His face turned chalky gray.

"No, Mr. Low!"

"One ...."

I could sense the crew watching.

"Two ...."

The kid's eyes stretched wide!

I lifted the Colt .45 to the bridge of his nose and tensed, as if ready to press the trigger.

"Thhh...."

"Don't fire," he shrieked, "I'll do it. I'll do it."

I could have collapsed, but strove to appear composed.

"Just one more time, Mr. Low. Just one more time. Okay?"

"Okay, McNutt." We turned to attack.

The promise to McNutt didn't count. The important thing was to get back into action.

Personnel from an English flak boat, its deck bristling with skyward-pointing anti-aircraft guns, waved as we passed. But what of the enemy? They'd either shifted positions or had had enough, and dropped back. In any case, we couldn't locate them.

And then, bullets again impacted our hull. Exhausted after having been hit so many times, and shaken by McNutt's fear, I decided to get beyond enemy machine gun range to await Lieutenant Garver's instructions. It wasn't long before he radioed.

"Sequence a barrage."

"Can't do it. I have only a few rockets left, and those damn machine guns are going to kill us."

"Call for naval gunfire."

"NGLO's dead and his corporal doesn't know how. We have contact because you were locked-on when NGLO got hit."

"Lieutenant Scott's dead?"

"Yeah, dead."

After an almost palpable pause, Garver rejoined, "Call Navy aircraft."

The corporal shrugged his shoulders. "Don't know how."

"Lieutenant," I said, "I'm going to semaphore that British ack-ack boat to unload on the strong point. Can you spot it, right off the point?"

"Roger," he replied.

"If you see those Brits lowering their guns, take cover."

"Roger wilco. Garver, standing by."

"Rocket boat thirteen standing by."

Cervone was so excited that he forgot what little semaphore he knew. Flags in hand, I stood on the foredeck and in simplistic, but to the point, semaphore signaled, "Roar, Lion, roar."

I watched officers on the ship's bridge as they considered my message. Shortly, orders were given and stanchions and rails were set aside so that gun barrels could be depressed to horizontal. An anti-aircraft barge designed to protect invaders from air attack skimmed thousands of shells into the German's fortification. Fireballs cascaded hundreds of feet upwards, with them marker puffs, tracers, and huge clouds of dirt and sand.

The tombstone of smoke mushroomed from the earth. All who saw it were awestruck. Those enemy still alive surrendered.

I nudged the boat to shore. First Lieutenant Garver and his troops greeted us warmly. We'd been partners, we'd created death in three dimensions. It was all about us, in the air we breathed. We shared a sad, gruesome, morbid and perhaps dishonorable, camaraderie.

Agape at the ruination, I asked, "How many did you lose?"

"About thirty. So long, Navy," Garver said. "We head inland now."

I felt sick. I felt like a murderer. I felt heroic. My battle report proposed a citation for each of my crew. As for McNutt, I recommended a study for battle fatigue. Interrogating officers asked much about our part in the invasion, but McNutt's name was never mentioned. I don't know what happened to him or to my men, as shortly thereafter we were separated.

THE UNITED STATES OF AMERICA

TO ALL WHO SHALL SEE THESE PRESENTS, GREETING:

THIS IS TO CERTIFY THAT
THE PRESIDENT OF THE UNITED STATES OF AMERICA
HAS AWARDED THE

PURPLE HEART

ESTABLISHED BY GENERAL GEORGE WASHINGTON
AT NEWBURGH, NEW YORK, AUGUST 7, 1782
TO

LIEUTENANT ALBERT MELVIN LOW, U. S. NAVAL RESERVE

FOR WOUNDS RECEIVED
IN ACTION

AUGUST 15, 1944

GIVEN UNDER MY HAND IN THE CITY OF WASHINGTON
THIS eighteenth DAY OF December 19 Fifty-six

In time, I was awarded the Silver Star, the second highest award the Navy can bestow, the first being the Navy Cross. The citation was signed for the President by the Secretary of the Navy. Later, I was awarded a second citation signed for the President by Admiral H.E. Hewett, Commander of the Unite States Eighth Fleet. Admiral Stark, Commander of the United States Forces in Europe, awarded me the Commendation Meal. Captain Timmerman honored me with an individual citation. Acknowledgement from Lieutenant Eggar and the hate group would soon be coming.

APA-13/P16

U.S.S. JOSEPH T. DICKMAN
℅ Fleet Post Office,
New York, N. Y.

18 August, 1944.

From: Commanding Officer, U.S.S. ▓▓▓▓▓▓
To :   Ensign Albert Melvin Low, D-V(G), U.S.N.R.

Subject: Commendation.

1.   Your Commanding Officer has been informed by the Boat Group Commander, that your performance of duty during recent amphibious operations has been very commendable. He reports specifically that:

"During amphibious operations on the coast of Southern France, 15 August, 1944, Ensign Albert Melvin Low, D-V(G), United States Naval Reserve, during his patrol activities with the Naval Gunfire Liaison Officer aboard his LCS, directed his craft within 100 yards from the beach taking an enemy machine gun under fire, and only withdrawing to give first aid to his coxswain who was hit in the eye by an enemy bullet. While his task was only to direct the fire of the close support destroyers, LOW also semaphored an idle LCG, giving it directions for firing on an enemy battery in the hills beyond the beach, thus effectively further assisting in the neutralizing of enemy shore fire."

2.   Your Commanding Officer considers your conduct and performance of duty as setforth in the foregoing to have been praⁱworthy, and hereby takes pleasure in commending you highly therefor.

3.   One copy of this letter is being forwarded to Bureau of Naval Personnel, with the request that it be filed your official records.

Silver Star Medal

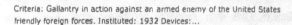

Criteria: Gallantry in action against an armed enemy of the United States
friendly foreign forces. Instituted: 1932 Devices:...

The President of the United States takes pleasure in presenting the SILVER STAR MEDAL to

LIEUTENANT, JUNIOR GRADE, ALBERT MELVIN LOW
UNITED STATES NAVAL RESERVE

for service as set forth in the following

CITATION:

"For conspicuous gallantry and intrepidity as Officer in Charge of a Support Boat in action against the enemy during the amphibious invasion of Southern France in August 1944. While rendering close-range fire support to the initial assault wave, Lieutenant, Junior Grade, (then Ensign) Low handled his boat with great skill and determination and, despite wounds sustained from enemy machine-gun fire, maneuvered his boat within point-blank range of hostile artillery, successfully silenced one enemy strong point with concentrated rocket and machine-gun fire and materially assisted in the total destruction of two others, thereby contributing substantially to the early and secure establishment of the beachhead. His courage and devotion to duty were in keeping with the highest traditions of the United States Naval Service."

For the President,

To protect the privacy, and years before this book was conceived, Albert Low changed the names of all officers and some crewmen when he wrote his memories of Utah Beach and Southern France.

Southern France, 6:00 a.m., August 15, 1944
Gunner Clinton E. Birch, "Hero's Hero"

Memories of my father Clinton E. Birch, Sr., by Clinton Birch, Jr.
My father is still alive as I write his memoir. His medical disposition at 81 has left him unable to write in his own hand. I have thus undertaken to write his memories down as he spoke them to me over the years. I am further compelled to convey his story after receiving the draft copy of this book and finding out he was part of the "Quintessential Rocket Boat Crew" of Ensign Albert M. Low and after researching his naval records, which he kept; finding out he was a hero's hero at the Southern France, Invasion, August 15, 1944 and received a major "Commendation" there that day; a commendation that has made our family proud and should be recorded in this book as corroboration of Ensign Albert M. Low's summary, which precedes this, and for naval history and posterity. The Commendation is listed on the following page.

My father was born in Readsboro, VT, on June 27, 1926. He graduated from eighth grade, and worked on the family farm daily. He did not enjoy farming and at 17 he wanted to enlist in the Navy. Seventeen-year-olds needed the signature of their parents and, after much resistance, his father signed. He enlisted in the Navy on September 30, 1943. He trained in Sampson Naval Academy in Sampson, NY. He completed his training in Little Creek, VA, in March 1944 in the new Secret Rocket Boat Program. After the war, he met his wife, Barbara, and produced nine children, twenty grandchildren, and twenty-two great grandchildren. He never became a rich man, but he was a good provider. He taught us by example to not be afraid of a little hard work, as he often maintained two jobs. Besides logging, he worked at Specialty Paper Mill in Monroe Bridge, MA, first as a worker, then as the mill supervisor, before he retired in 1985.

He never spoke much of D-Day at Utah Beach and his Rocket Boat missions with Ensign Albert M. Low, like many in his generation, but grieved over the number of Army and Navy men's bodies they had to pick up out of the water and transport to the larger ships for identification. After reading Albert M. Low's summary at Utah Beach, I see he was involved in death defying attacks against batteries along the beach and cliffs.

At Southern France, he did recount to my mother and [me], corroboration of Albert M. Low's actions in removing the coxswain from his post after having his eye shot out and nose partially shot off and other crew members being wounded along with his officer in charge, Albert M. Low. My father's recount of his own actions, "When I took control of the 30-caliber machine gun, I had to duck, because I could see the water dancing toward me and I knew it wasn't raining, it was lead. When I got back up, the gun wouldn't fire because the ammo belt had been shot off."

His commendation on the next page best summarizes his bravery and courageous contributions to his crew and country at Southern France, August 15, 1944. I am proud of my father and know that he played a big role in the success of the allies that day and the winning of the war. My

)7.

F2c. Clinton E. Birch

Gunner on Ensign Albert M. Low's, Rocket Boat Crew

File No.
P15

UNITED STATES EIGHTH FLEET

Serial: 6043

23 December 1944

From: Commander United States EIGHTH Fleet.
To :   Clinton E. Birch, Seaman First Class, U. S. Naval Reserve.

Subject: Commendation.

1.   Your outstanding performance of duty while serving as a crew member of a support boat during the amphibious invasion of Southern France in August 1944 is considered worthy of special commendation.

2.   You performed your duties with skill and fearless determination when your boat was engaged in rendering close-in fire support for the initial assault wave. You courageously remained at your post despite heavy enemy machine gun fire at point-blank ranges, which caused two other members of the crew of your boat to be wounded. By your calm and dependable action and disregard for your own safety, you materially assisted in the silencing of three enemy strong points, thereby contributing substantially to the rapid weakening of enemy resistance and to the early and secure establishment of the beachhead.

3.   I commend you for your exceptional courage and outstanding devotion to duty, which reflected credit upon yourself and the Naval Service.

4.   You are hereby accorded the privilege of wearing the commendation ribbon pursuant to the authority delegated by ALNAV 179.

H. K. HEWIT

In Reply
Refer to
Serial
APA-13/P16

U.S.S. JOSEPH T. DICKMAN

℅ Fleet Post Office,
New York, N. Y.

18 August, 1944.

From: Commanding Officer, U.S.S. JOSEPH T. DICKMAN APA-13.
To :   FORD, William L. (609-24-25), Sea .1c., USNR.

Subject: Commendation.

　　1.   Your Commanding Officer has been informed by the
Support Boat Officer of LCS(S) #16 that your performance of duty
during recent amphibious operations has been very commendable.
He reports specifically that:

　　"During amphibious operations in the Mediterranean
Area, 15 August, 1944, FORD, William Lowell, (609-24-25), Sea.1c.,
United States Naval Reserve, was in LCS(S) #16, in charge of the
.50 Cal. machine guns, in an opposed landing on the coast of
Southern France. His fire against enemy strongpoints and in support of the pre-assault waves was both accurate and effective. His
efficiency and hard work contributed to the ultimate success achieved by the initial assault waves."

　　2.   Your Commanding Officer considers your conduct and
performance of duty as setforth in the foregoing to have been most
praiseworthy and hereby takes pleasure in commending you highly
therefor.

　　3.   One copy of this letter is being forwarded to the
Bureau of Naval Personnel, with the request that it be filed with
your official records.

R. J. MAUERMAN.

File No.
P15

UNITED STATES EIGHTH FLEET

Serial: 5 04   23 December 1944.

From: Commander United States EIGHTH Fleet.
To :   William L. Ford, Seaman First Class, U. S. Naval Reserve.

Subject: Commendation.

　　1.　　Your outstanding performance of duty while serving as a crew member of a support boat during the amphibious invasion of Southern France in August 1944 is considered worthy of special commendation.

　　2.　　You performed your duties with skill and fearless determination when your boat was engaged in rendering close-in fire support for the initial assault wave. You courageously remained at your post despite heavy enemy machine gun fire at point-blank ranges, which caused two other members of the crew of your boat to be wounded. By your calm and dependable action and disregard for your own safety, you materially assisted in the silencing of three enemy strong points, thereby contributing substantially to the rapid weakening of enemy resistance and to the early and secure establishment of the beachhead.

　　3.　　I commend you for your exceptional courage and outstanding devotion to duty, which reflected credit upon yourself and the Naval Service.

　　4.　　You are hereby accorded the privilege of wearing the commendation ribbon pursuant to the authority delegated by ALNAV 179.

H. K. HEWITT

CHAPTER 10

Evolution
of the
Rocket Boat Program for the Invasion of Japan

(1) Phase out of the 36' LCS(S) Rocket Boat Program
(2) Phase in of the 203' LSM(R) Rocket Carriers, LCI(R)s, and LCM(R)s

Ensigns Harry W. Tennant & Herman F. Vorel

Evolution of the Rocket Boat Program

Ensign Harry W. Tennant

Ensign Harry Waldon Tennant was born on November 9, 1918 in Bath County, VA. He graduated from Berea College in Berea, KY, with a degree in Business Administration in 1943. He became a management engineer in Logistics and Construction for the federal government; a multi-government classified program. He married Ethel Shrader in 1943. They had four children. He retired in 1975 in Naples, FL.

By D-Day, as several of the other original officers, he was separated from the Rocket Boat Program and became CO/Officer in Charge of a Destroyer Command U.S. Europe Yacht, (an elegant 47' mahogany yacht leased to the Navy by Barbara Stanwick). All Gunnery batteries and all ships in and around Plymouth were to be in readiness for an anticipated German V-2 missile attack. On June 3, 1945, the Destroyer Commander ordered this yacht to his command in Weymouth by sundown. Our mission was completed, and bags of secret materials (covering D-Day Operations) were delivered to navy officials. I was next ordered to LST307 as Gunnery Officer and Watch Officer for D-Day, and crossed the English Channel 104 times in the next few weeks, to enhance the allied Invasion of France with materials, men, equipment, and supplies.

Ensign Harry W. Tennant

The 36' LCS(S) Rocket Boat Program had been pretty successful in several categories: first, in stealth. It was small enough—36'—in that it was a very hard target to hit with the artillery of the day; German 75-mm and 88-mm cannons. Also, the boat was flat bottom and road only four-feet deep. The average torpedo ran six feet or greater under the water, so it was not sinkable by any submarine. The twin fifty calibers and two thirty-caliber machine guns were like a "hornet's nest," per Ens. Albert M. Low, when concentrated, and could "match or best" just about any incoming artillery. The smoke screening capability only augmented its stealth attributes, being undetectable after delivering rockets and heading back to its transport. As for its main objective—obliteration of machine gun batteries, land mines, fortified houses, and pillboxes—very few officers were able to obtain the results that Ens. Albert M. Low and his crew did via utilization of his boat with the Naval Gunnery Liaison Officer; NGLO, a spotter on a battleship, collaboration with the army on the beach and the joint effort capability to systematically knock out six strong points at Utah Beach. One reason for the need for greater enhanced technology, along with a different, much greater deployment strategy, was for the onerous, dreaded Invasion of Japan.

The primary mission of delivering rockets was evolving to bigger boats with 100 or more rocket launchers, such as the 203' LSM(R), picture below, and the LCI(R) and LCM(R)s, to deliver a much more concentrated and powerful result with bigger rockets than we had on the LCS(S). This concentration of rockets, of course, delivered from a greater distance from the beach, assuring saving lives; the LCS(S) had gone within 200 to 300 feet of the beach, with casualties.

Ensign Harry W. Tennant

My assignment to an LSM(R) as Commanding Officer was immediate after hostilities ended in Europe in May 1945. I was to return once again to Little Creek, VA, Amphibious Training Base and recruit and train a crew of four officers and 70 personnel. Next, I left for Orange, TX, to take command of an LSM(R). I believe this duty was given to me because of my earlier rocketry training in Solomons, MD, and my experiences in ship handling in the English Channel. LSM(R) 188 below is similar to the one I was to command.

LSM(R)-188

My ship LSM(R) was being outfitted in Orange Texas when the Atomic bomb attack ended all Navy war assault operations against Japan. Harry Tennant

LSM(R)-188

- LSM(R)-188 class Landing Ship, Medium (Rocket):
- Displacement: 968 tons (loaded)
- Length: 203'6'"
- Beam: 34'6'"
- Draft: 5'6" - 5'9'"
- Speed: 13.2 knots (max, loaded)
- Armament: 1 5"/38 DP, 2 40mm, 3x1 20mm; (#188-195): 75 4-rail Mk. rocket launchers; (#196-199): 85 Mk. 51 automatic rocket launchers
- Complement: 5 officers, 76 enlisted
- Capacity: 5 medium or 3 heavy tanks, or 6 LVTs or 9 DUKWs.
- 2 GM 1440 BHP @ 720 rpm (each) diesels, twin screws
- Converted while building from LSMs
- Built at Charleston Navy Yard, and commissioned 15 November 1944

Before we could take over the Rocket Ship LSM(R) in Orange, TX, the atomic bombs were dropped on Hiroshima and Nagasaki, ending the planned invasion of Japan and the war. Ensign Harry W. Tennant

Ensign Herman F. Vorel

After termination of my duties in Marseille, France in October 1944, I was transferred from my beloved LCS(S) Rocket Boat to a larger Rocket Launcher LCI(R) 763, below. We were being trained for the Final Invasion—the Big One—The Invasion of Japan. Our LCI(R) was built for the big punch of rocketry to support and knock out the Japanese War Machine. Below is an actual picture of my LCI(R). Lots of Rockets, with specifications alongside.

USS *LCI(R)-* 763

- Landing Craft, Infantry (Rocket):
- Displacement: 385 tons (full load)
- Length: 160'4"
- Beam: 23'3"
- Draft: 2'8" forward, 5'0" aft (landing)
- Speed: 15.5 knots
- Armament: 1 40mm, 4 20mm, 6 5" rocket launchers
- Complement: 3 officers, 31 enlisted
- 8 GM diesel engines, twin screws

My LCI(R)763 in route for Japan, 1945

Ensign Herman F. Vorel

Unfortunately, a big typhoon beached us and we were out of commission. Then the big bombs were dropped in Japan and the war was over.

OCKETEERING
A Legal Practice Among Men of Wo

(U. S. Navy foto via A.P. Wirefoto)

ASSAULT and battery cases—loaded with rockets—cover the sides of an LCM. The rockets, cheaper than artillery shells, fill the bombardment gap between the initial barrage and troop landings.

(Navy foto via A. P. Wirefoto)

↑ **TROUBLE IN THE AIR**

A Navy LCM puts three volleys of rockets into the air, all within a split second, during test operations. Object of maneuvers was to coordinate firepower with amphibious landings.

LCM(R)s ready to pack their punch in Japan

Luckily, the war was over and full utilization of these heavy duty rocket launchers never materialized. All Rocket Boat Operations temporarily ceased.

Thank God, and God Bless America!
Ensign Herman F. Vorel

ABOUT THE BOOK

D-Day, June 6, 1944—a day never to be forgotten. More than 156,000 troops crossed the English Channel from England to Normandy, making it the largest seaborne invasion in history. Leading the pre-invasion ashore were the brave, but little known, rocketboatmen, as they called themselves. Their job, as the first close up Naval offense, was to soften up the German beach defenses with 48 rockets, machine gunnery, and smoke screening, preparing the way for the LCVP infantrymen.

Through private diary entries and firsthand accounts, many read here for the first time, the unfolding of the earliest events leading up to the invasion is told in vivid and unforgettable detail. In choppy seas, oftentimes like sitting ducks in the water, these young men manned their landing craft approached the beaches at exactly 6:00 A.M.— half an hour before H-hour—unleashed their barrage of forty-eight rockets, twelve boats at Omaha, twelve at Utah Beach, lighting up the coastline like a Fourth of July grand finale. Several boats actually beached at Omaha and Utah under shell and bombardment and crossfire sustaining casualties, eliminating German coastline pill boxes.

Relive their compelling tales in this incredible story.

ABOUT THE AUTHOR

Inspired by the altruistic nature of his father, Ensign William H. Palmer, a birth-rite Quaker from Stoudsburg, PA, and his voluntary service to his country in World War II, William Howard Palmer, Jr., brings us firsthand accounts of the brave young men who sometimes wore fear on their sleeves but forged ahead in spite of it, paving the way for, perhaps, history's greatest military invasion.

An MBA graduate from Fairleigh Dickson University in Teaneck, New Jersey, Mr. Palmer is a retired Business Manager from the Paramus Veterans Home in Paramus, NJ. This father of three, originally from Paramus, New Jersey, now makes his home in Washingtonville, New York.

Mr. Palmer was formerly involved as a little league manager for ten years and an EMT with the Blooming Grove Volunteer Ambulance Corps for seven years. He enjoys writing, fly fishing, and skiing in his spare time. He has also published articles in Civil War Times magazine.

CPSIA information can be obtained
at www.ICGtesting.com
Printed in the USA
LVHW020839291022
731799LV00007B/301